Understanding Your
MUSLIM NEIGHBOR
Moving from Fear to Love

—

Robert D. McCroskey

𝔣

THE FOUNDRY
PUBLISHING

Copyright © 2017 by Robert D. McCroskey
The Foundry Publishing
PO Box 419527
Kansas City, MO 64141

ISBN 978-0-8341-3602-1

Cover Design: J.R. Caines
Interior Design: Sharon Page

Scriptures marked (KJV) are taken from the King James Version.

Scriptures marked NASB are from the *New American Standard Bible®* (NASB®), copyright © 1960, 1962, 1963, 1968, 1971, 1972, 1973, 1975, 1977, 1995 by The Lockman Foundation. Used by permission. www.Lockman.org.

Scriptures marked NIV are from the *Holy Bible, New International Version®* (NIV®). Copyright © 1973, 1978, 1984, 2011 by Biblica, Inc.® Used by permission. All rights reserved worldwide.

Library of Congress Cataloging-in-Publication Data
Names: McCroskey, Robert D., 1946- author.
Title: Understanding your Muslim neighbor : moving from fear to love / Robert D. McCroskey.
Description: Kansas City, Mo. : The Foundry Publishing, 2017. | Includes bibliographical references.
Identifiers: LCCN 2017017838 (print) | LCCN 2017017480 (ebook) | ISBN 9780834136021 (pbk.) | ISBN 9780834136069
Subjects: LCSH: Christianity and other religions—Islam. | Islam—Relations—Christianity. | Islam—Doctrines.
Classification: LCC BP172 .M378 2017 (ebook) | LCC BP172 (print) | DDC 261.2/7—dc23
LC record available at https://lccn.loc.gov/2017017838

The Internet addresses, email addresses, and phone numbers in this book are accurate at the time of publication. They are provided as a resource. The Foundry Publishing does not endorse them or vouch for their content or permanence.

10 9 8 7 6 5 4 3 2 1

CONTENTS

—

ABBREVIATIONS FOR QUR'AN TRANSLATIONS

—

Ahamed *English Translation of the Meaning of the Quran.* Translated by Syed Vickar Ahamed. Lombard, IL: Book of Signs Foundation, 2005, https://muslimsforallah.com/quran-english-translation-syed-vickar-ahamed/.

Ahmed Ali *Al-Qur'an.* Translated by Ahmed Ali. Princeton, NJ: Princeton University Press, 1994, https://www.amazon.com/Al-Quran-Contemporary-Translation-Ahmed-Ali/dp/0691074992#reader_0691074992.

Dawood *The Koran.* Translated by N. J. Dawood. 1956. Reprint, London: Penguin Books, 2006, https://www.amazon.com/Koran-Penguin-Classics-N-Dawood/dp/0141393831/ref=sr_1_1?ie=UTF8&qid=1491239142&sr=8-1&keywords=the+koran+dawood#reader_0141393831.

al-Hilali *Interpretation of the Meanings of the Noble Quran.* Translated by Muhammad Taqi-ud-Din al-Hilali and Muhammad Muhsin Khan. Houston: Dar-us-Salam Publications; Riyadh, SA: Darussalam Publishers and Distributors, 2007. All rights reserved. http://www.noblequran.com/translation.

Pickthall *The Quran.* Translated by M. Pickthall. Islam 101. http://www.islam101.com/quran/QTP/.

Shakir *The Holy Qur'an.* M. H. Shakir. Flushing, NY: Tahrike Tarsile Qur'an, 1983, http://quod.lib.umich.edu/k/koran/browse.html.

Yusuf Ali *The Meanings of the Holy Qur'an.* Translated by Yusuf Ali. Islam 101. http://www.islam101.com/quran/yusufAli/index.htm.

INTRODUCTION

—

"The tree of fear grows in the land of ignorance." This intriguing phrase appears at the opening of a book on evangelical Christianity in America.[1] Interestingly, the author, Muhammad Arif Zakaullah, is a Muslim who teaches economics at a university in Malaysia. Commenting on another person's religion is always risky, and to do so as a foreign observer is even more difficult. Yet Zakaullah was so motivated to eliminate ignorance about Americans in general, and Christians in particular, that he was willing to undertake that arduous task.

In many ways, my purpose in writing this book is the same as Zakaullah's. My wife and I served as missionary teachers in Indonesia for thirty-eight years. You may be surprised to learn that Indonesia is the fourth most populous country in the world, and the overwhelming majority of its people are Muslims, which makes Indonesia the largest Muslim nation on earth. Over the years, we developed many friendships with the Muslims living all around us, and we discovered many positive aspects of their faith. We also experienced firsthand what it was like to live as a minority—ethnically, nationally, and religiously. Most of the time we were accepted as different but equal. However, from time to time problems arose because of our neighbors' ignorance of our Christian beliefs. Sometimes we were accused of doing things that were detrimental to the well-being of the various communities where our denomination had churches. We saw pastors threatened by their Muslim neighbors. At other times we encountered walls of suspicion and misunderstanding simply because we were different.

My wife and I have returned to our native country, where we once again live as members of the majority culture. Though many would dispute the idea that the United States is a Christian nation, I notice that many political candidates in the country proudly identify their affiliation with a Christian church, knowing it will garner many votes and lose few. Though Islam is growing in America, Muslims still constitute a minority and are often viewed with suspicion—just as my wife and I sometimes were in Indonesia.

Yet Christians, Muslims, and Jews have something important in common: We all claim Abraham as our spiritual father. Jews and Christians believe we are children of Abraham through Abraham and Sarah's son, Isaac. Muslims also believe that they are children of Abraham—but through Abraham and Hagar's son, Ishmael. The Qur'an (sometimes spelled Koran), the primary religious text of Islam, repeatedly refers to Jews and Christians as "people of the book," signifying that we share common scriptures. As we will see, Islam accepts the validity of large portions of both the Old and New Testaments.

We, in fact, have a great deal in common with our Muslim neighbors. Yet our basic human nature is to categorize the people who don't look like us, act like us, or share our faith as being *other*. Our natural reaction is to build a wall of separation between them and us. Thus unfolds a chain of negative responses born out of ignorance: Ignorance creates prejudice, prejudice leads to suspicion, suspicion produces fear, fear ignites hatred, and hatred breeds violence. Indeed, "the tree of fear grows in the land of ignorance."

Just as Zakaullah tried to explain Christianity to his fellow Muslims, I aim to explain Islam to my fellow Christians. I also write as an outsider. However, my years of living in Indonesia have given me a sympathetic perspective on Islam that I invite my Christian friends to share. Because the chain of negative response begins with ignorance, understanding is the key to breaking that chain. So my goal is to help other Christians build bridges of understanding toward our Muslim neighbors.

We will begin by learning about the chasm that too often divides Muslims and Christians. Part I will trace the history of Islam, which is inseparable from the life of the prophet Muhammad. Next, we'll identify the sources of authority that underscore the Muslim faith, and understand the way Muslims think about religious matters. Finally, we will identify the major sources of contention between Muslims and Christians.

Part II moves us into the foundations for building our bridge of understanding. We will identify the general points of commonality between Islam and Christianity and learn three particular beliefs that are, if not identical in both faiths, at least similar enough to be familiar. These concepts—intention, holiness, and struggle—will serve as strong planks for building our bridge of understanding.

In Part III we get practical, learning specific strategies that will help us reach out to Muslims in our schools, workplaces, or communities. You will gain the confidence to begin a relationship that can, with God's help, become a close and enriching friendship.

Christianity and Islam are the two religions in this world with the largest number of followers. Thirty percent of the world's population currently identifies with Christianity, and Islam is close behind at 25 percent. Islam is also the world's fastest-growing faith. If current trends continue, Islam will be the largest religion in the world within twenty years. Clearly, if the world is to be at peace, Christians and Muslims must be at peace.

I write with the hope that this book will be a step in the direction of peace. May it inspire you to breach the walls of fear and hatred that too often characterize our relationships with Muslims; may it encourage you to build a bridge of hope based on understanding. Let us begin a new chain of responses that will lead from understanding to acceptance, from acceptance to appreciation, from appreciation to respect, and—ultimately—from respect to love.

Part I

The Chasm between Us

1
WHO ARE THE MUSLIMS?
—

If a new family moved in next door, you would probably have lots of questions about them. Who are they? Where did they come from? Why did they choose to live here? Do they have relatives nearby? You would likely want to hear a bit of their story.

In the same way, you may have many questions about your Muslim neighbors. Who are the people called Muslims? How did this religion originate? What accounts for the different sects within Islam?

The first step in getting to know any neighbor is to learn more about that neighbor. So our first step in building a bridge of understanding to our Muslim neighbors is to hear their story, to find out who they are, and to learn how their faith has developed over the last fourteen centuries.

The historical account contained in this chapter is the story of Islam as believed by most Muslims. However, as with any story, alternative versions exist. The same is true for the story of Christianity. For example, some people love the message of Jesus but believe he was merely a human being who lived an exceptional life. They do not believe in miracles, and they say the Bible is an instructive book that does not have divine authorship. Most Christians believe something quite different, however. We believe that Jesus is the Son of God, who rose from the dead, and that the Bible is the divinely inspired Word of God. Similarly, many Western scholars have taken a critical view of Islam, casting doubt on the historicity of Muhammad as well as the formation of the Qur'an. But my purpose here is not to argue history or theology. My aim is to tell the story of Islam as understood by millions of faithful Muslims around the world. When we are finished, you will understand the basic outline of Muslim history and the major branches of the Muslim family tree. In this chapter we will trace the beginnings of the Muslim story from the time of creation through the life of the prophet Muhammad.

As we move through the story, be alert for similarities and differences between Islam and Christianity. You will likely be able to note many of each. Some of the differences have become chasms that breed prejudice and suspicion. The similarities can become supports for our bridge of understanding.

For most of this chapter, I will tell the story through the eyes of a Muslim. Remember, our purpose here is not to debate the historical or theological validity of this story but simply to present it as Muslims themselves understand it.

The Prehistory of Islam

There is only one God, and he has had only one message for humankind since the very beginning. The Qur'an states that there has never been a people to whom God did not send a prophet carrying his message: "And there never was a nation but a warner had passed among them" (Qur'an 35:24, al-Hilali), and "For every *Ummah* (a community or a nation), there is a Messenger" (Qur'an 10:47, al-Hilali). God's message is simple: All people must acknowledge God as the great Creator and submit to his will and his commandments. In fact, the word *islam* means "submission," and a *muslim* is one who has submitted to God. While most translators understand Qur'an 22:78 to say that God was the one who coined the word *muslim*, some commentators understand this verse to say that Abraham coined this term.

Adam was the first one to submit to God (and, therefore, to become a Muslim). Adam was also the first in a long line of prophets bringing God's message to humanity. Belief in these prophets is a cornerstone of Islamic faith. There are three levels of messengers from God.

Prophet (Nabi). A prophet is one who has received a revelation from God and is commissioned to share this revelation with people. Opinions vary as to the total number of prophets sent by God, but general thinking accepts that there were 124,000, of whom 25 are named in the Qur'an. These include Adam, Noah, Abraham, Moses, David, Elijah, Elisha, Ezekiel, Jesus, and Muhammad.

Apostle (Rasul). An apostle is one who has received not only a revelation from God but also a sacred book and a commission to teach God's law (*shari'a*). Lot, Ishmael, Jethro, Hud, Salih, Noah, Abraham, Moses, Jesus, and Muhammad are all apostles.

Prophets of Firm Resolve (Ulu al-'azm). These could be considered super prophets, those who showed great power and persistence in their mission. They are Noah, Abraham, Moses, Jesus, and Muhammad.

As the various apostles came with their revealed books and laws (*shari'a*), they replaced the previously revealed books and laws. Muhammad is called the Seal of the Prophets (see Qur'an 33:40) because, with him, the line of prophets has been sealed— or closed. He is the final prophet. Since Muhammad's God-given book has been perfectly preserved in its original state, there is no further need for a revealed book.

The Time of Ignorance (*Jahiliyya*)

Jahiliyya means "days of ignorance." It refers to the time prior to the revelation of the Qur'an through the prophet Muhammad, when people lived in ignorance of God's laws.

Prior to Muhammad's time, Mecca was already a well-known city in Arabia. It was a center of both trade and idol worship and home to the *Ka'aba*, a cube-shaped structure with a black stone embedded in the eastern corner of its foundation. Various explanations have been offered for the origin of this sacred stone, perhaps the most interesting being that it is a meteor that fell to earth and was incorporated into this shrine, making the stone a link between the *Ka'aba* and the heavens.[1] The *Ka'aba* is thirty-three feet wide, forty feet long, and forty-nine feet high. It is hollow on the inside, with a door in the northeastern face. According to some Islamic traditions, Adam built this structure, and God lifted it up during the flood from which Noah was spared. By Abraham's time, the *Ka'aba* had fallen into disrepair. At some point, Abraham journeyed south to Mecca, where Ishmael and Hagar lived, and Abraham and Ishmael rebuilt the *Ka'aba* together.[2]

Islamic tradition suggests that people recognized that the *Ka'aba* was the shrine to Allah, whom they considered the chief god. However, people mistakenly honored a variety of other gods, represented by idols enshrined within this cubed structure. The *Ka'aba* housed 360 idols, including representations of Allah's supposed daughters, al-Lat, al-Uzza, and al-Manat.

Arabs from across the Arabian Peninsula made *hajjes,* or "pilgrimages," to the *Ka'aba* to honor these gods. Many of the practices of these early worshippers were later incorporated into the ritual of Islamic pilgrimages (see chap. 4). These include throwing pebbles on heaps of stone, circumambulating the *Ka'aba*, running between two hills in symbolic search for water (*sa'y*), kissing and stroking holy stones, and observing sacred periods of time.

Another significant aspect of the *jahiliyya*, and one that deeply impacted Muhammad's life, is the importance of poets and their words. As is common in tradition-focused cultures, language and power went together. Sometimes the heroes of the battlefield were not the swordsmen but the poets. There are stories of vast armies that turned away in despair after a great poet shamed them. These tales are reminiscent of the way Goliath used taunts to keep the army of Israel cowering in their tents (see 1 Sam. 17:10–11) and of how Sennacherib surrounded Jerusalem, trying to discourage the Israelites with his words so they would just give up (see Isa. 36).

Muhammad later used this concept of the power of words to validate his prophethood. When he came, claiming to be a prophet of God, the Jews living in Arabia said that if he were a genuine prophet, he would be able to do miracles, as Moses and Elijah had done. In response, Muhammad pointed to the Qur'an as his miracle. He challenged his detractors to produce a *sura* (chapter) as powerful as those found in the Qur'an (Qur'an 10:38), but none could. Therefore, Muslims perceive that the Qur'an itself is the great validating miracle of the prophet Muhammad. This doctrine is known as the *i'jaz*, or "inimitability," of the Qur'an.

Though the age of *jahiliyya* formally ended with the coming of Muhammad, the concept is reinterpreted by some modern-day Muslim reformers[3] who believe many of today's Muslims are living in an age of ignorance because they do not live in accordance with God's laws.

The Life of the Prophet Muhammad

The emergence of Islam as a religion,[4] while it has roots deep in antiquity, actually begins with the appearance of Muhammad in Arabia in about the sixth century CE. The traditional date for Muhammad's birth is 570 CE, and the place is Mecca in the Arabian Peninsula.

Ancestry, Birth, and Early Life

Muhammad's full name was Muhammad ibn 'Abdullah ibn 'Abdul-Muttalib. The word *ibn* means "son of," so his name was

Muhammad, son of 'Abdullah, son of 'Abdul-Muttalib. Muhammad's mother's name was Amina. Lineage is very important for Arabs, and Muhammad's lineage has been carefully traced.

Quraysh
|
Qussay
|
'Abd Manaf
|
'Abd Shams—**Hashim**—Nawfal—al-Muttalib

Umayyad rulers 'Abdul-Muttalib
|
al-'Abbas — 'Abdullah — Abu Talib
| |
'Abbasid rulers **Muhammad**

Two names in this family tree have great significance. The first is Quraysh. In the years following Muhammad's life, there was a strong sentiment that leadership of the Muslims should always fall to a member of the Quraysh clan. The second important name is Hashim. Over the years, many of the rulers in Muslim lands claimed legitimacy because they were descendants of Hashim. The Hashemite kingdom of Jordan is one example. 'Abd Shams and al-'Abbas are also of note because the first two early kingdoms of Islam were led by descendants of these men.

Arabia is a desertlike land with harsh conditions, so it was essential during Muhammad's time that everyone, even city dwellers, learn to survive in the countryside. Children from the cities were often sent to live with rural families so they could be taught to thrive in the land of their birth. As a child, Muhammad spent a couple of years with an adoptive family in the area of Taif.

Muhammad's father died before he was born, and his mother died when he was just six years of age. The boy was taken in by his grandfather, 'Abdul-Muttalib, but 'Abdul-Muttalib died only two years later. So at the age of eight, Muhammad went to live with his father's brother, Abu Talib. Abu Talib was a merchant and caravan trader. Mecca was a center for trade, with two great caravans departing each year. One traveled south in the winter, to Yemen, to trade with ships coming from India. In the summer, another went north to Syria, to trade with the Byzantines. On one of these trips to Syria, when Muhammad was with the caravan, the travelers met up with a Christian monk named Bahira. Bahira noticed something different about this caravan. A cloud seemed to be following it, providing shade for the people and camels. When the caravan stopped, Bahira met all the people in the caravan, but none piqued any interest. He asked if there was anyone else in the company, and the caravanners said there was a small boy watching over the animals. When the boy Muhammad was brought forward, Bahira recognized him as a special person. He removed the boy's shirt and found a mark on his back that attested to his uniqueness. Bahira told Abu Talib that his nephew was destined for greatness but that some would try to kill the child, so Abu Talib must protect him.

At a young age, Muhammad rose to a prominent position in the caravan trade. He quickly earned a reputation as an honest merchant. A well-to-do widow named Khadija took notice of Muhammad and let it be known that if he were to propose, she would not turn him down. Before long, the two were married. Muhammad was twenty-five, and Khadija was fifteen years his senior. There is some question about Khadija's age because the couple produced seven children together—four girls and three boys. All of the boys died in infancy. By all accounts, the marriage was a very happy one.

Revelations

Muhammad had always been a pensive person and frequently went to a mountain cave called Hira, near Mecca, where he meditated and fasted. In the year 610, on what is called the Night of Decree, or the Night of Power (Qur'an 97:1), Muhammad received his initial revelation, brought to him by the angel Gabriel (*Jibril*). This initial revelation is recorded in Sura 96:1–5. Muhammad was told to "Read! In the Name of your Lord, Who has created" (Qur'an 96:1, al-Hilali). However, the incident terrified Muhammad, and he hurried home to his wife, asking her to cover him up. He explained what he had just experienced, saying he didn't know if this was a vision from heaven or something from Satan. Khadija assured him it was from God and, for further proof, brought him to see her uncle, Waraqa ibn Naufal, who was a Christian. Waraqa ibn Naufal agreed that this surely must be a divine experience.

Over the next twenty-three years, Gabriel periodically appeared to Muhammad, revealing more and more of the Qur'an. For his part, Muhammad began preaching the message he had received. He began his ministry shortly after receiving the initial revelation. Muhammad's ministry is divided into two parts— twelve years in his native Mecca, followed by ten years in Medina. The central theme of Muhammad's preaching was that God is one, having no partners, no equals. This doctrine is called *tawhid*, or the "unicity of God." When Muhammad broadcast this message to his fellow Meccans, he included a severe condemnation of their idol worship at the *Ka'aba*. He preached about a blissful paradise awaiting those who submit to God and live righteously and a terrible hell awaiting those who reject God.

Opposition in Mecca

The people of Mecca did not respond well to Muhammad's message. Much of their livelihood was derived from the religious pilgrims who worshipped at the *Ka'aba*. Their response to Muhammad was similar to that of Demetrius and the silversmiths to the apostle Paul in the city of Ephesus (see Acts 19). In the face of this opposition, Muhammad continued to preach, stressing the unicity of God. One by one, he began to attract converts. Many of them were from the lower stratum of Meccan society, but some were not. Khadija was one of his first and staunchest supporters. Another was his nephew, 'Ali, who lived in Muhammad's home. Muhammad's uncle Abu Talib, head of the Hashim clan, was also a strong supporter, though he never became a believer. The other Meccan clans repeatedly complained about Muhammad and begged Abu Talib to withdraw his umbrella of protection so they could silence Muhammad. Abu Talib refused.

The Satanic Verses and the Night Journey

One day when Muhammad was preaching to the resistant Meccans, he told them that although there is only one supreme God, the three goddesses al-Lat, al-Uzza, and al-Manat could be prevailed upon to make intercession to God on behalf of those who prayed to them (Qur'an 53:19–20). The Meccans gladly received this news, for it signaled a major change in Muhammad's teaching. This new doctrine opened the door to the worship of other gods. Later Muhammad considered what he had said and realized the implications of this new doctrine. Before long he received a new revelation from Gabriel, nullifying this earlier statement (Qur'an 53:23). Muhammad realized that these earlier verses had been not been inspired by God but were a temptation from Satan—hence, they are referred to as the Satanic Verses.

Toward the end of Muhammad's Meccan ministry, as persecution was increasing, he had a two-part experience known as the Night Journey ('*Isra*') and the Ascension (*Mi'raj*). Muslim scholars disagree on whether this was a literal event or simply a vision. In

any case, tradition declares that Muhammad made a night journey from Mecca to the Farthest (*al-Aqsa*) Mosque, in Jerusalem,
which led to the construction of the al-Aqsa Mosque on the site
of the Temple Mount after the city fell under Islamic rule. There,
he mounted a flying horse and ascended into the heavens. He visited seven levels of heaven, each with its own guardian saint(s).
The guardian of the first was Adam; the second, Jesus and John;
the third, Joseph; the fourth, Enoch; the fifth, Aaron; the sixth,
Moses; and the seventh, Abraham. There was still a higher level,
which was the abode of God. Gabriel, who had accompanied him
thus far, told Muhammad he would have to approach the final
level by himself; Gabriel could go no further.

Thus tradition teaches that Muhammad met with God and,
among other things, heard from him the requirement for daily
prayer by Muslims. After talking with God, Muhammad descended, arriving at Moses's level. Moses asked what God required of humankind, and Muhammad replied that Muslims should pray fifty
times a day. Moses assured him that was too much and told Muhammad to go back to God and bargain for a lower requirement.
So Muhammad returned to God, and just as Abraham bargained
for the salvation of Sodom and Gomorrah, Muhammad bargained
with God to reduce the number of daily prayers. Each time Muhammad went to God, God lowered the requirements by ten, and
each time Muhammad returned to Moses, Moses said it was still
too much. Finally, on Muhammad's sixth visit, God reduced the
number from ten to five. Moses contended that it was still too much,
but Muhammad replied that he was embarrassed to ask for fewer
than five. Thus the number of daily prayers was set at five.

Escape to Medina

In 619 two of Muhammad's strongest supporters died within
days of each other. The first was his uncle Abu Talib, who had

extended to him the clan's protection from the hostile Meccans. The second was his beloved Khadija. She had been the first to accept her husband's message and had been his confidante for many years. Muhammad took no other wives during her lifetime. According to all reports, they had a strong and mutually supportive marriage.

Abu Talib was replaced as the head of the Hashim clan by Abu Lahab, who is specifically mentioned in the Qur'an as being doomed to the fires of hell. From the beginning of Muhammad's ministry, Abu Lahab was antagonistic to him. Abu Lahab withdrew the protection of the Hashim clan from Muhammad, leaving him defenseless against his many enemies. Muhammad knew that if he stayed in Mecca, he would surely be killed.

At that same time, Muhammad received overtures from a delegation from Medina (originally known as Yathrib), a farming oasis located two hundred miles north of Mecca, to come to their city as an adjudicator between conflicting tribes. The city was home to two Arab tribes, the Aws and the Khazraj, who feuded constantly.[5] In addition, there were three Jewish tribes that called Medina home: the Qurayza, the Qaynuqa, and the al-Nadir. So in 622, the Muslims began to leave Mecca in small groups to evade attention. Muhammad, his nephew 'Ali, and Abu Bakr were the last to leave. Abu Bakr was an early believer who would later be the first *khalif*, or "successor"[6] to Muhammad as leader of the Muslims.

The trek to Medina was long and dangerous. The journey is known as the *hijra*, and it marks year zero of the Muslim calendar. Muslim dates are denoted as AH, meaning *annō-hijra*.[7] The *hijra* is comparable to other definitive moments: Noah entering the ark of safety or the exodus of the Jews from Egypt to Palestine. For Christians, the birth, crucifixion, and resurrection of Christ are likewise defining, with AD, or *annō dominī* ("in the year of our Lord"), dating time from the traditional year of Christ's birth.

Battles with Mecca

About seventy-five Muslims emigrated from Mecca, and there were about that same number of Muslim converts already living in Medina. It was difficult to find a livelihood for the newcomers, so in order to bring in funds, Muhammad and his Muslims began to waylay Syria-bound caravans operated by the Meccans. In 624, to end this threat to their commercial interests, the Meccans responded by sending a thousand-man army, which met a much smaller army of Muslims at the wells of Badr. Though outnumbered, the Muslims achieved a great victory, which they perceived to be God-given. The following year, the two armies met again at the Battle of Uhud, and this time the Meccans prevailed. Muhammad himself was wounded in the fighting. Two years later the armies met again at Medina in what is known as the Battle of the Ditch, named for the moat that was dug in defense of the city. Weather and privations forced the Meccans to return home, and the Muslims again knew that God had intervened on their behalf.

When Muhammad came to Medina, he assumed the Jews there, being fellow monotheists, would recognize him as a prophet in the Jewish tradition and support him. The fact that they did not accept his status as a prophet meant that he quickly perceived them as an existential threat to his leadership. Muhammad's response to this threat is symbolized by his instruction to his followers to change the direction of their prayers from Jerusalem to Mecca. Muhammad began to suspect that the Jewish tribes were supporting his enemies in Mecca. As a result, he punished one of the Jewish tribes following each of his battles. After the Battle of Badr, the Banu Qaynuqa were expelled from Medina. They were merchants and craftsmen and were allowed to leave Medina with their wealth but forfeited their property. Following the Battle of Uhud, the Banu Nadir were expelled. They derived their wealth from palm groves and had to surrender ownership of their groves and leave empty-handed. As the siege of Medina took place during the Battle of the Ditch, Muhammad became convinced that the third Jewish clan, the Banu Qurayza, were conspiring to sneak the Meccans into the city. After the battle, Muhammad called upon Saʿd ibn Muʿadh, an elder of a tribe that had long been allied with the Banu Qurayza, to pass a verdict upon the behavior of the Banu Qurayza. Saʿd ordered the Qurayza to forfeit not only their wealth and property but also their lives and freedom. One by one the men of the tribe were beheaded, and the women and children sold as slaves.[8]

Muhammad's Wives

During this period, Muhammad began to accumulate wives. Though he had been monogamous during his marriage to Khadija, he began to marry again in 620. The exact number of his wives and concubines is disputed, but there were at least twelve and perhaps twice that number. Many of these wives were widows of Muslim fighters who had no one to take care of them. By marrying them, Muhammad agreed to support them.

Two of the wives in particular have caused much criticism among Westerners. The first is Zaynab bint Jahsh, who was married to Muhammad's adopted son, Zayd bin Haritha. Reportedly, it was not a happy marriage. Muhammad was attracted to her, and Zayd offered to divorce her so Muhammad could marry her, but this was culturally unacceptable. However, Muhammad received a revelation from God specifically allowing him to marry her (Qur'an 33:37–38).

The other problematic marriage was to ʿAʾisha, the daughter of Muhammad's good friend Abu Bakr. ʿAʾisha was six years old at the time of her marriage to Muhammad. Tradition says the marriage was not consummated until she was nine. ʿAʾisha became

Muhammad's favorite wife and is the namesake of many Muslim women today.

Final Years

After the Meccan wars, Muhammad continued to gain followers, which further isolated his enemies in the Quraysh clan. In 630, Muhammad and a huge group of Muslims descended on Mecca with the intent of performing the great annual *hajj* to the holy city. By this time the Meccans were so isolated that they opened the city gates to Muhammad, who came in as conqueror to the city from which he had fled in fear just eight years earlier. Over the next couple of years Muhammad gained control of the entire Arabian Peninsula through wars and treaties.

In 632, Muhammad performed the *hajj* to Mecca for the last time. During this trip the final verse of the Qur'an was revealed to him: "This day have I perfected your religion for you, completed My favour upon you, and have chosen for you Islam as your religion" (Qur'an 5:3, Yusuf Ali). Standing on the plain of Arafat, Muhammad delivered his final and most famous address to the Muslims, challenging them to always remember that they are brothers. He abolished usury and blood feuds among his people, proclaimed the rights of women and slaves, and closed his sermon with this proclamation: "Verily, I have concluded my mission! I have left among you a plain command, the Book of God, and manifest ordinances. If you hold fast to them, none of you shall go astray."[9]

Muhammad must have realized he was ill, for his final message had a valedictory tone. By the time he returned to Medina, he was feverish and confined to bed. Muhammad died about noon on June 8, 632, at age sixty-three. According to the Muslim calendar, he died on the same month and day as he was born.

An Ancient Faith

Thus Muslims perceive their tradition to be an ancient faith. From the beginning, God has revealed himself in various ways through prophets, apostles, and prophets of resolve—including Adam, Noah, Moses, Elijah, and Jesus. Each prophetic revelation supersedes the previous one, and Muhammad's revelations, recorded in the Qur'an, take precedence over all. Muhammad is the Seal of the Prophets, the last and greatest of God's messengers. With the life of Muhammad, God's revelation to humankind was closed, and Islam became something more than the doctrines of monotheism and submission to the laws of God: it became a religion.

When Muhammad left his home city of Mecca in 622, he was in fear for his life. He and his tiny handful of followers, numbering just 150, took refuge in the city of Medina. Within ten years, however, Muhammad had become the undisputed ruler of the Arabian Peninsula, and his followers numbered in the tens of thousands. Today, Islam is the second largest of the world's religions, claiming more than 1.5 billion adherents. In the next chapter, we will trace the growth of Islam as a world religion from the time of Muhammad to today, including a look at the major sects within Islam.

2
THE RISE OF A WORLD RELIGION

—

A change in the leadership of any organization can be a time of crisis. This is especially true when the leader was the founder or led for a long time—or both. Think of the early days of the Christian church. After Jesus ascended into heaven, the apostles faced the challenge of replacing one of their number, organizing themselves for ministry, making doctrinal decisions, and coping with the threat of persecution. The development of the church from the missionary travels of Paul, the church fathers, the Great Schism, the Middle Ages, the Crusades, and the Reformation is a fascinating story indeed. Though we may not be able to recall the entire story, each of us has some sense of where we fit in the Christian family tree.

Similarly, the Muslims, too, faced a series of challenges following the death of Muhammad, beginning with the choice of a *khalif,* or "successor" to the Prophet. In this chapter, we trace the continuation of their story. We will see the major developments within from the time of Muhammad to the present day. We will give particular attention to the following developments:

- The Rashidun Caliphs
- The Rise of Muslim Political Power

- Sects within Islam
- Radical Islam

Again, watch for similarities and differences to the Christian story. That will strengthen your understanding of Islam and increase your ability to dialogue with your Muslim neighbors.

The Rashidun Caliphs

Muhammad's death was a great shock to the Muslim community, which gathered in the mosque in disbelief. According to tradition, Abu Bakr addressed them, saying, "O people, whoso hath been wont to worship Muhammad—verily Muhammad is dead; and whoso hath been wont to worship God—verily God is Living and dieth not."[1] Muhammad had not clearly designated a successor. So the community chose his successor by means of a *shura*, a small council of respected Muslim leaders. This established a pattern that has been characteristic of Islamic rule. Succession of rule in Islam has seldom been hereditary until the postcolonial era. Instead, a *shura* is usually appointed to determine who is the wisest person among those considered eligible to succeed the previous ruler.

Succeeding Muhammad would turn out to be a difficult and dangerous job. Of his first four successors, only one died a natural death. The other three were assassinated, two of them by fellow Muslims.

The leader of the Muslims was known as the *khalif* or, more commonly in English, *caliph*. The first four caliphs collectively are known as the *Rashidun,* or Rightly Guided Caliphs. These four are fondly viewed as the Patriarchal Caliphs, and their combined rule of twenty-nine years was the golden age of Islam. Each of the first four caliphs was related to Muhammad through marriage. Here is a summary of their rule.

Abu Bakr

Abu Bakr led the Muslims from 632 to 634. His daughter 'A'isha was Muhammad's favorite wife, making Abu Bakr a father-in-law to Muhammad. Abu Bakr's greatest achievement was the consolidation of Muslim control over the Arabian Peninsula. Many Arab tribes felt that with Muhammad's death, they could pull out of the Muslim tribal alliance. Abu Bakr prevented this and added some two hundred thousand square miles to Muslim territory. Abu Bakr died of natural causes in 634.

Umar

Umar succeeded Abu Bakr and led the Muslims from 634 to 644. Umar also was a father-in-law to Muhammad through his marriage to Umar's daughter Hafsa. Under Umar's leadership Islam's armies were highly successful, and the Muslim empire grew to encompass Syria, Iraq, Persia, and Egypt. Umar added some 1.5 million square miles to Muslim-held lands and has been called the true founder of the Muslim state. He was assassinated by a Persian slave.

'Uthman

With the selection of 'Uthman (r. 644–56) as caliph, rule reverted to the Umayyad clan of Mecca, a clan who were late to accept Muhammad's rule. 'Uthman married two of Muhammad's daughters; first Ruqayya, and, upon her death, Um Kulthum. He was seventy years old when selected as caliph, and he promptly replaced many able leaders with members of his own Umayyad clan. Under his reign, Muslim expansion continued through North Africa and Afghanistan, adding some eight hundred thousand square miles to Muslim-controlled lands. 'Uthman's most important accomplishment was commissioning the compilation of one official Qur'an and destroying all variant copies. This version of the Qur'an is known as the *'Uthmanic recension*, and Muslims today believe the Qur'an they hold in their hands is identical to it. 'Uthman was assassinated by disgruntled Muslim soldiers.

'Ali

After feeling he had been passed over three times for selection as caliph, 'Ali finally was chosen to succeed 'Uthman. He reigned from 656 to 661. 'Ali was married to Muhammad's youngest daughter, Fatima. He was fifty-five years of age when chosen as caliph, and his brief reign was marked by constant conflict with the Umayyad clan. 'Ali was assassinated by renegade Muslims known as the Kharijites.

The Rise of Muslim Political Power

When Muhammad died, Muslims controlled about 1 million square miles of territory. That territory expanded rapidly under the leadership of the Rashidun Caliphs, who added some 2.5 million square miles. Several of the ruling dynasties were large and noteworthy.

The Umayyads: 661–750

'Uthman, the third caliph, was a member of the Umayyad clan. This clan descended from 'Abd Shams, who was a brother of Muhammad's great-grandfather. The Umayyads were disliked by many Muslims for two reasons. First, they had been among the strongest opponents of Muhammad during his early Meccan ministry. Second, when they managed to get 'Uthman, one of their own, elected caliph, he was accused of nepotism because he systematically placed family members in positions of authority and leadership throughout the Muslim lands.

One of 'Uthman's relatives, Mu'awiya, was governor of Syria. When 'Uthman was assassinated and 'Ali succeeded him, Mu'awiya demanded that 'Ali seek out the persons who had assassinated his kinsman and bring them to justice. When Mu'awiya realized that 'Ali would not do so, he took up arms against him. Later, when 'Ali himself was assassinated, Mu'awiya gained control of the Muslims, and thus was born the Umayyad dynasty, which lasted ninety years. One of Mu'awiya's first acts was to move the capital of the Muslim empire from Medina, in Arabia, to the city of Damascus, Syria.

During the reign of the Umayyads, Muslim armies swept westward through North Africa and into Spain, and northeastward through present-day Iraq and Afghanistan. They also seized control of large sections of India in the south. By 715, the Islamic empire stretched from Spain to the borders of China.

In October 732, exactly one hundred years after the death of Muhammad, a significant battle took place in Poitiers, France, that became a turning point in both Islam and Christianity. Muslim forces dispatched by the governor of Spain were defeated by the Frankish army led by Charles Martel. This battle denotes the high-water mark of Muslim expansion into "Christian" Europe. As Mark Noll puts it, "While it is possible to exaggerate the decisive influence of this one battle, it is also true that Charles Martel, as well as his successors, came to be seen as the saviors of Europe."[2] It took another seven hundred years for Christian forces to finally drive the Muslims out of Europe, but the tide had turned at Poitiers.

The Umayyad reign was marked by turmoil and discontent. The martyrdom of Husayn (680), the grandson of Muhammad, early in the Umayyad rule, was an event from which this ruling community never fully covered. We will look closer at that event in a moment when we learn about the development of the Shi'a.

The 'Abbasids: 750–1258

The 'Abbasids claimed to be more closely related to Muhammad than the Umayyads. The 'Abbasids were descendants of al-'Abbas, who was an uncle of the Prophet.

The 'Abbasids rose to power aided by the support of those who favored 'Ali and were dismayed over the fate of his son, Husayn. However, once they were in power, the 'Abbasids abandoned their pro-'Ali stance in favor of the Sunni. (We'll talk more about the Sunni in just a moment.) The 'Abbasids moved the capital of the Muslim world east, to Baghdad, favoring Persian over Arab influences.

The Crusades stand out as the most significant event of the 'Abbasid period due to their historical significance and modern impact. The Crusades were an attempt by European Christians to "rescue" the Holy Land from its "imprisonment" by Muslims. Seven crusades were dispatched from Europe, starting in 1098 and ending in 1250.

Evaluated according to their stated intent—to free the Holy Land from Muslim domination—the Crusades were not a long-term success. The crusading kingdoms of the Holy Land lasted, with one brief intermission, from 1099 to 1291. At the time, most Muslims were unconcerned about the Crusades, viewing them as a local problem for Muslims in the Levant. Most Muslims were far more concerned about the rise of the Mongols in the east than with Christian knights in the west. The heartland of the Muslim empire, centered on Baghdad, was untouched by the conflict.

However, the idea of the Crusades is indelibly imprinted on contemporary Christian-Muslim relations. Muslims frequently refer to the aggression and cruelty of the Christian West during the Crusades. During recent years, some Christian leaders have publically apologized to Muslims for the actions of Christians during the Crusades. The Crusades continue to color the attitude of many Muslims toward the West in general and Western involvement in the Middle East in particular.

The 'Abbasids ruled the Muslim world for over five hundred years. That reign is generally divided into three periods:

- Glory and Expansion: 750–861
- Corruption: 861–1094
- Political Decadence and Decline: 1094–1258[3]

The end, when it came, was brutal. The Mongols, led by Hulagu, the grandson of Genghis Khan, captured Baghdad in 1258. He ordered the caliph al-Musta'sim beaten to death, then massacred an estimated three-quarters of the 2 million residents of Baghdad, which at the time was considered the greatest city on earth.

Middle Ages to the Present

For centuries the 'Abbasids had permitted their generals to carve out increasingly independent areas of rule; dynasties such as the Idrisids, the Buyids, and the Seljuks were permitted to exist with only nominal recognition of the caliph in Baghdad. However, the overthrow of the 'Abbasids marked the formal end of a united Muslim empire. Since that time, no single political entity has controlled the entire Muslim world. During the period following the 'Abbasids, three Muslim empires stand out either for their scope or for their longevity.

The Safavid Empire: 1501–1736. The Safavid Empire was founded by Shah Ismail I and was centered in Iran. This was a Shi'ite kingdom, which permanently marked Iran as a Shi'ite country.

The Mogul Empire: 1526–1862. This empire ruled India. Its founder was a descendant of Timurlane and the great Mongol leader Genghis Khan. The famous Taj Mahal is a lasting monument to this empire. In the end, British influence forced the Moguls to retire.

The Ottoman Empire: 1453–1924. The Ottoman Empire, centered in Anatolia (the Asian part of modern Turkey), was the most extensive of all three empires. Their first century was a time of great success and expansion. After centuries of pressure and attacks from the surrounding Muslims, the great Christian bastion of Constantinople fell. The Muslims continued their advance in all directions as Hungary, Syria, Egypt, Algiers, and Greece all fell to Ottoman forces. Their tide turned in 1529 with an unsuccessful siege on the city of Vienna. With the great awakening of Europe, the advance of Islam halted and a slow, centuries-long decline began. By the nineteenth century, the Ottoman Empire was known as the "sick man of Europe." On March 3, 1924, the caliphate was abolished in favor of a secular presidency.

Sects within Islam

Although some Muslims might suggest that Islam has no denominations and that all believers are part of a common Muslim community (*umma*), there are, in fact, several major sects within Islam, and there are pronounced differences between them. From the time of Muhammad himself, religious and political authority has been intertwined in Islam. So it is not surprising that the development of branches or sects within the Muslim faith cannot be separated from Muslim political history. Here are the three most significant communities within Islam: *Shiʿite, Sunni,* and *Sufi.*

The Shiʿa

When Muhammad died with no one designated as successor, there were differences of opinion about who should take leadership. Some felt that the next leader had to come from the Quraysh tribe in Mecca. Others felt it needed to be a companion who had been closely associated with Muhammad during his life. Still others were convinced that the successor should come from Medina because that city had done so much to establish the Muslims. A particularly strong faction felt that the immediate successor should be a blood relative of Muhammad, specifically his nephew 'Ali, who had grown up in Muhammad's household. They became known as the *Shi'atu 'Ali* (party of 'Ali) and were finally called *Shi'a*. Because the Shi'a believe Muhammad wanted 'Ali to succeed him, many have rejected the first three caliphs as usurpers.

When 'Ali died, Mu'awiya, an Umayyad, seized control of the Muslims. When Mu'awiya died, his son Yazid took control. However, many Shi'a continued to support the 'Ali family claim to leadership. A group of Shi'a in Kufa (a city in modern Iraq) sent word to 'Ali's son Husayn, promising him their support. Husayn decided to seize the throne and made his way from Mecca toward Kufa. Yazid heard of the plan and sent an army to intercept Husayn's small band. They met on the plain of Karbala. Several days of negotiations ensued, while Yazid's army stood between Husayn's band and the river. Meanwhile, none of the promised aid from Kufa materialized. On October 10, 680, Yazid's forces killed Husayn and his entire band, including infants. This day is known as *'Ashura* and is the most holy day in the Shi'ite calendar. On *'Ashura*, the Shi'a vow to avenge the faithlessness of their Kufa compatriots. So from its earliest days, Islam has been split between the Shi'a and the non-Shi'ite.

The Sunni

In the early years of Islam, a number of groups divided from the main body over a variety of issues. The majority of Muslims, however, rejected these divisions and began to identify themselves as "Not Shi'ite" or "Not Mu'tazilite." In time, they became known as the "people who follow the *sunna* (example) of the Prophet and the Majority." This name was simplified to *Sunni*. The Sunni are by far the largest sect within Islam, comprising some 85 to 90 percent of all Muslims. However, exact numbers cannot be known due to the doctrine of *taqiyya*. Because the Shi'a have always been a minority and their relations with the Sunni have been marked by violence, the doctrine of *taqiyya* allows Shi'a to conceal their identity. Iran is a majority Shi'ite country, and there are significant blocks of Shi'a in Iraq, Syria, India, Pakistan, Lebanon, and Kuwait. However, the number of Shi'a living elsewhere is difficult to determine.

The Sufis

Sufism is a third branch of Islam. Sufis are the mystics of Islam, and their religious outlook falls somewhere between the Christian view of God as loving and immanent (close by) and the classic Muslim view of God as transcendent (distant) and authoritative.

The theologies of both the Sunni and the Shi'a emphasize the transcendence of God, a characteristic recognized by Jews and Christians too. However, Christians also view God as being close by, since he came to dwell with humankind in the person of Jesus Christ. Muslims do not accept Jesus as God, so their theology does not teach the immanence of God in Christ. If the most prominent attribute of God from the Christian viewpoint is love, the most prominent attribute of God from the Muslim standpoint is the will of God. So classic Muslim theology does not talk about the nearness and love of God but instead emphasizes the majesty and commands of God. Sufism was a response to this void.

When the companions and friends who had personally known Muhammad died, storytellers kept the early history of Islam alive. These storytellers went from place to place, telling stories of Muhammad and quoting his revelations. They were mostly ascetics who dressed in coarse wool called *suf*, hence the term *Sufi*. There is a broad spectrum of practice within Sufism, from those who quietly meditate on the Qur'an to the Whirling Dervishes of

Rumi, but the common characteristic is an emphasis on the inner aspects of one's relationship to God.

Sufis believe there is an outer, exoteric meaning of the Qur'an that is clear to everyone but there is also an inner, esoteric meaning that is hidden to all except one who has special knowledge (*ma'arifa*). One of their favorite verses is, "We are nearer to him than his jugular vein!" (Qur'an 50:16, al-Hilali). There is an often-cited story in which God says, "I was a Hidden Treasure, and I loved to be known, and so I created the world."[4] The concepts of love, heart, and motive are central to the Sufi understanding of God. Sufi thought is captured well by this prayer by Rabi'a al-'Adawiyya (717–801 CE), a former slave who became an influential teacher: "O God, if I worship You in fear of Hell, burn me in Hell, and if I worship You in hope of Paradise, exclude me from Paradise; but if I worship You for Your own sake, withhold not from me Your everlasting beauty."[5]

The Sufis established religious orders similar to Christian monastic orders, called *tariqa*. Each of these orders is led by a teacher who is called a *shaykh* or *pir*, and each member advances through a series of stages in which the disciple learns disciplines such as patience, fear, thanksgiving, love, and hope. Most of these disciplines begin with repentance and end with annihilation or losing one's self in the greatness of God.

Radical Islam

Western observers often understand little about the sects within Islam or their historical and theological differences. What Westerners generally perceive is that some Muslims want peace and others want war. My wife and I were living in Indonesia when the September 11 attacks took place. It was hard to understand how people could do such a thing while shouting out "*Allahu ak-bar*," which means "God is great." In Indonesia, we immediately began to see bumper stickers proclaiming, "Islam is a religion of peace." Many Muslim friends expressed sorrow and sympathy to us. So how can it be that some could commit atrocities in the name of their religion, while others could be shocked and saddened by the same events?

Let's start by recognizing that members of any religious group will have other affiliations or viewpoints that color their interpretation of scripture and their faith. Within Christianity, for example, a person may be a member of a denomination such as Catholic, Methodist, or Nazarene, yet layered on top of those distinctions are movements such as fundamentalism, Pentecostalism, evangelicalism, and liberalism. Beyond those identifications are political and social identifiers such as Republican, Democrat, Libertarian, and Tea Party. And there are substrata within those distinctions: liberal Democrat, moderate Republican, fiscal conservative, social liberal, and the like. So within Islam there are Sunni and Shi'a, but there are also classifications such as fundamentalist, moderate, and liberal.

One group, known as the *Salafiyya* movement, has garnered much Western attention. The term comes from the phrase *al-salaf al-salih*, which means "pious forefathers."[6] The *Salafiyya* movement holds that Muslims are not living up to God's standards. This group longs to return to the golden age of Islam. They want to go back to the days of Muhammad and the Rashidun.[7] Some have labeled this movement as fundamentalist. Here are ten key characteristics of *Salafiyya* thought:

1. *A literal interpretation of the Qur'an.* They interpret every verse in the Qur'an literally, not recognizing any context that might mitigate or influence the meaning of a verse.

2. *Rejection of scriptural criticism.* Related to their literal interpretation of the Qur'an is the view that it may not be subjected to critical thought or analysis.

3. *Dependence on divine revelation.* They reject the use of human reason and instead depend solely upon divine revelation for arriving at truth.

4. *Demand to reinstate shari'a law.* They wish to eliminate the distinction between church and state, recognizing only God's laws. This would include the use of religious police to ensure compliance with *shari'a* law.

5. *Renunciation of Western imperialism in all of its forms*—political, cultural, economic, religious, and ideological.

6. *A call for a more just society and a fairer distribution of wealth.*

7. *Refusal to acknowledge historical progress.* This movement longs for the "good old days" of seventh-century Arabia.

8. *Advocacy for revolution in the name of religion.*

9. *Claim of absolute truth.* They reject all other viewpoints, including all other religions, claiming that only they are right.

10. *Blame for the world's ills on a third party.* An ever-present theme among proponents of the *Salafiyya* movement is that all problems encountered in Islamic countries are caused by someone else, usually Israel and the United States.

To achieve these goals, members of this movement are willing to take extreme measures, including the use of violence. Thus the 9/11 hijackers were proponents of the *Salafiyya* ideology, and it was the moderates of Indonesia who responded with the claim that "Islam is a religion of peace." Both believe they represent the true Islam, and both can find Qur'anic support for their positions.

A Religion with Political Might

The history of Islam is intertwined with the political history of the Middle East. Muhammad himself was a political leader, and his immediate successors vastly expanded the territory under Muslim control using both warfare and treaties. Inevitably, that expansion brought violent clashes with other faiths, notably with Christianity in Europe. The Sunni (majority) and Shi'a (minority) branches of Islam have also clashed, sometimes violently. Muslim political expansion was curbed after the Battle of Poitiers in 732; however, powerful Muslim states have continued to exist throughout North Africa, the Middle East, and parts of Asia. Today, most Muslims are diverse theologically and politically. While the vast majority of Muslims do not support the expansion of Muslim influence through violence, a small but powerful minority does hold this aim. In the next chapter, we will dig deeper into the Muslim mind, learning how Muslims think by examining their sources of religious authority—beginning with the Qur'an.

3
HOW MUSLIMS THINK

—

One way of understanding any group of people is to examine their history. Where do they come from? What significant events have shaped their identity? How did they come to exist as the people they are today? Those questions deal mostly with historical events, and as we've seen, the history of the Muslim people centers on Muhammad but was significantly shaped by the leaders and events that came after his death. Today, Islam is the second-largest world religion, comprising some 1.5 billion people. Some fifty nations have a majority Muslim population, and there are Muslims living in virtually every country of the world. Though the major Muslim sects are Sunni, Shi'ite, and Sufi, most attention today is given to the *Salafiyya* movement, which cuts across sectarian lines and advocates a return to the golden age of Islam.

A second way of understanding the Muslims is to examine how they think. What makes them tick? What matters to them? Where do they get their theology? What we are really asking is this: From what sources do Muslims derive their beliefs? Or what are their sources of authority? When we know the answer to that question, we will have a basis for dialoguing with our Muslim neighbors on matters of faith.

What do we mean by sources of authority? Let's use the Christian sources of authority as a point of comparison. The rallying cry of the Protestant Reformers of the sixteenth century was *Sola scriptura,* meaning that "only Scripture" was authoritative for them. That is true of many Protestants today—the Bible is their primary source of truth. However, other Christians, such as the Eastern Orthodox, also consider the teachings of the apostles as handed down through the creeds and traditions of the church to be authoritative. While the creeds might be secondary to Scripture, they are in agreement with the Bible and more clearly state our beliefs on certain points—such as the deity of Christ. So the creeds also have some authority in defining our faith, as do the traditions of the church. Roman Catholics also recognize the pope as an authoritative source. Followers of John Wesley speak of the Wesleyan quadrilateral—Scripture, tradition, experience, and reason—as four sources of authority. While our human reasoning might not be equal to Scripture, it is a valuable tool for discerning truth. Pentecostals and some others also view the ministry of the Holy Spirit as a source of authority, so what the Spirit reveals through conscience, awakenings, or dreams may be highly authoritative to some Christians.

So what are the Muslim sources of authority? How do Muslims determine what is true? There are several authoritative sources of truth for Muslims, and they are separated into three levels of importance.

Primary Sources

The Qur'an

The Qur'an is the foundation stone for Islam. A Muslim understanding of the place of the Qur'an in Islamic tradition encompasses both a Christian understanding of the Word of God revealed in Scripture and the understanding of the Word of God "made flesh" (KJV) and eternally "dwelling among us" (NIV) in Christ (John 1:14).

The Qur'an was revealed by the angel Gabriel to Muhammad in several stages over a period of twenty-three years beginning in 610. Some believe that Muhammad was illiterate, so when Gabriel revealed passages, Muhammad memorized them and recited them to his followers, who wrote them down. Two key doctrines are important for understanding how Muslims view the Qur'an.

I'jaz. The word *i'jaz* means "inimitability." Muslims believe no other book can compare with the Qur'an in its beauty and style. When people questioned Muhammad's claim to be a prophet, citing the fact that he had done no miracles, Muhammad asserted that the Qur'an itself was the highest miracle and proof of his authenticity. He challenged his detractors to produce a chapter like those found in the Qur'an (2:23) and claimed that neither man nor spirit could produce anything equal to it (17:88).

Most Christians hold to the *dynamic theory of inspiration* of the Bible, meaning that God revealed his truth to human beings who wrote the messages filtered through their own history, culture, and personality. Though the Bible was written over a period of about fifteen hundred years and was obviously composed by a number of hands, the overall message is consistent. As Paul writes, "All scripture is given by inspiration of God" (2 Tim. 3:16, KJV).

Muslims hold to a *mechanical dictation theory of inspiration* of the Qur'an, meaning that Gabriel dictated God's words to Muhammad, who memorized and recited them word for word. Thus, the words of the Qur'an are believed to be the *exact same words* spoken by Gabriel. Ibn-Khaldun, a great philosopher of the Middle Ages, contended that the Qur'an is far superior to the Christian and Jewish scriptures for this very reason: it contains the exact words of God, not the ideas of God expressed by human beings.[1]

Qadim. The second key doctrine regarding the Qur'an is its *qadim*, or "eternality." One of the early sects of Islam, the Mu'tazilites, contended that if God was one and could have no equal or no partner, the Qur'an could not be an eternal book but must have been created in time and space. To believe otherwise, they felt, made the Qur'an an equal partner with God because it always existed. The argument between the traditionalists, who believed the Qur'an was eternal, and the Mu'tazilites, who believed it was created, was fierce, but the traditionalists eventually won.

According to Muslim understanding, there was a threefold *descent* of the Qur'an. The Qur'an began as the *protected tablet* (85:21–22), residing in the highest heaven with God. Then the Qur'an was transmitted to the lowest heaven during the Night of Majesty, when Muhammad first began to receive God's revelation in 610. Finally, over the twenty-three years of revelation to Muhammad, the Qur'an was transmitted to humankind.[2]

The Qur'an is the highest authority for most Muslims, just as the Bible is for most Christians. They believe that it is God's last and greatest revelation and that it is incomparable and eternal. Muslims hold the Qur'an in extremely high regard.

The Hadith

A *hadith* is a story about the life and the practices of Muhammad, his companions, and the early successors to the Prophet.[3] Muslims use these stories as a means of interpreting the Qur'an and determining proper actions for a Muslim. This includes even the most ordinary things. For example, many Muslims today use a twig to clean their teeth because that was Muhammad's habit. From the *ahadith*, Muslims learn the things Muhammad did, forbade doing, or permitted by his silence on the subject.

Muhammad is viewed by Muslims as the Seal of the Prophets, the prophet who corrects the errors in transmission from all prophets who preceded him. Therefore, his example is the best guide for understanding and applying the Qur'an today. From an Islamic perspective, the life of Muhammad was the perfect picture of how God wanted human beings to live. We can recover that divine model by studying the behavior of Muhammad and his successors, as well as those companions who knew him. One Muslim writer expressed it this way: "The Prophet functioned as the projection of the divine message embodied in the Koran. He was the living commentary . . . intricately related to the silent text. Without the Prophet, the Koran was incomprehensible, just as without the Koran, the Prophet was no prophet at all."[4]

This is not a foreign idea for Christians, who believe that Jesus is the perfect example of a human life. After his death and resurrection, his apostles wrote the story of his life in the Gospels, including the things he both did and commanded, and tried to emulate him.

With the passing of generations after the death of the Prophet, it became increasingly important to find means to authenticate these stories about the example of the Prophet and the early companions. Increasingly, the *ahadith* of Muhammad were privileged over those of his companions and successors. Within a couple of centuries from Muhammad's death, there were hundreds of thousands of stories about Muhammad in circulation within the Muslim community. Many individual scholars began the task of collecting and organizing these stories. Over the centuries, Islamic tradition came to canonize six of these collections of *ahadith*, of which the most famous and respected were Bukhari and Muslim. The ninth-century *hadith* collectors went all over the early Muslim world collecting *ahadith*. Each *hadith* is composed of an *isnad*, which contains the record of transmission of the story, as well as the story itself. The *isnad*, or "record of transmission," must show the names of each person responsible for transmitting the story until it was reduced to text in a written collection. The quality of a *hadith* is assessed as much on the character of the transmitters as on the objective content of the narrative. If any individual in the chain of transmission is reputed to have been unsound in the practice of Islam or in moral character, the *hadith* is discredited. *Ahadith* are classified as *sound*, *good*, or *weak*. Bukhari is said to have collected some six hundred thousand different stories, which he culled to fewer than eight thousand to include in his collection.[5]

Secondary Sources of Authority

Muslims agree that the Qur'an and the *ahadith* cannot contradict one another. However, given the huge number of *ahadith* that exist, in practice, many such contradictions can be found. For example, the Qur'an specifies that a thief must have his hand cut off (5:38), but there is a *hadith* stating that Muhammad said this penalty could be waived if the theft was an inconsequential amount. So how are these two rulings to be made compatible? Also, what should be done in cases where both the Qur'an and the *ahadith* make no mention of a subject? To decide questions like that, Muslim jurists turn to two secondary sources: *Ijma‘* and *Qiyas*.

Ijma‘

Ijma‘ means "consensus." If a Muslim judge was faced with a problem where the Qur'an and the *ahadith* are either silent or contradictory, the judge could poll other judges to see what their understanding would be. Though not precisely the same, this practice bears some comparison to the Christian consensus that has been gained through the historic church councils, which clarified Christian beliefs.

Qiyas

Qiyas means "analogy." The principle of *qiyas* allows a judge to make a ruling in a case where the Qur'an speaks about a similar, though not exactly equivalent, situation. For example, the Qur'an says that slander besmirches the reputation of a virtuous woman and specifies how that should be addressed. But does slander also besmirch the reputation of a virtuous man? There was nothing in the Qur'an about that. However, in the exercise of *qiyas*, a judge could decide that if the penalty for slandering a virtuous woman was thirty lashes, that penalty could also be applied to the slander of a virtuous man. In utilizing *qiyas*, the judge had to use his reasoning power. This reasoning was called *ijtihad*.

Within a short time, Sunnis decided that all possible wisdom had already been discovered, and they "closed the door" to *ijtihad*. From then on it was the job of a Sunni jurist to study the decisions of his predecessors and to copy them. He was never to use his own power of reasoning to come up with a new or novel decision. This is not the case among Shi'a Muslims. The supreme spiritual leader, the ayatollah, has the authority and responsibility to use reasoning to discover new solutions for new problems.

Third-Level Sources

If we were to think of the Qur'an and the *ahadith* as something similar to the Law and the Gospels, and the *ijma'* and *qiyas* as something like the traditions and doctrines of the church, the third-level sources of belief would be like gospel music and a "word from the Lord." They represent the folk religion of Islam. Remember that the average Muslim probably cannot read Arabic, so the contents of the Qur'an are a mystery. A Muslim may have heard a few of the *ahadith*, but they don't play a large role in the formation of that Muslim's worldview. But there are other things that intimately affect the life of the average person in the Muslim world. These third-level sources of authority may powerfully shape the thinking of the average Muslim.

Previous Scriptures

Muslims accept parts of the Jewish and Christian Scriptures. They believe that God has been consistent in his revelation from the beginning to the end. So in as far as the Pentateuch, Psalms, and Gospels do not contradict the Qur'an, Muslims accept them as an authentic expression of God's will and as authoritative for Muslims.

Teachers (Shyakhs) and High Priests (Ayatollahs)

Both Sufis and Shi'a recognize the authority of teachers and priests. Their opinions and rulings carry much weight among their followers. Particularly important among these teachers are those who propagate traditions from one of the four great schools of Islamic law that developed in the early centuries of Islam. Those schools are the Maliki, Hanafi, Shafi'i, and Hanbali. Each possesses its own tradition of commentary on the Qur'an and the *ahadith*. Most Islamic communities adhere to one of these traditions of law.

Saints

In folk Islam, the veneration of saints is a significant practice. People commonly make pilgrimages to the tombs of saints in order to pray and seek God's help and blessing. They believe the tomb of a saint will lend power to their petition.

The Spirit World

In folk Islam, the spirit world has great influence. Witchcraft, ghosts, demons, *jinn*, hallowed or haunted places or things, amulets and talismans, spells, and counterspells are frequent objects of belief among common people.

Jinn. According to the Qur'an, angels are created from light. They are good and do God's bidding. Humans are created from clay or dust (Qur'an 55:14; 38:71). They can do God's will but often forget and commit sins. *Jinn* are created from fire (Qur'an 55:15). They can do good but also bad. Satan was the first *jinn*. However, not all *jinn* are bad. In fact, Muhammad was sent to remind both humans and *jinn* about God's commands (Qur'an 51:55–56), and at least one group of *jinn* who heard Muhammad's message were convinced of its truth and believed (Qur'an 72:1–2). The English word for *jinn* is *genie*, which, thanks to cartoons and television, is a well-known concept in the Western world.

Witchdoctors, Spells, Amulets. In folk Islam, the use of witchdoctors, spells, and amulets is common. A Muslim might consult a witchdoctor over anything from seeking a husband to curing an illness or passing a test.

Hallowed and Haunted Places. In Indonesia, banyan trees are considered sacred. Sometimes in the middle of a forest you will come upon a banyan tree with a white picket fence surrounding it. One of our churches in Indonesia met in a rented house that was believed to be haunted; no one else would live in it.

Dreams and Visions

The apostle Paul was converted after he saw a vision on the road to Damascus. Muslims, too, put great stock in dreams and visions. They believe that through them the human plane intersects with a spiritual plane and important truths are imparted. When we planted one of our first churches in a large city in Indonesia, a man began attending and later told that he had had a dream in which he saw a white man coming to his city and he was told to accept what this person had to say.

A Spectrum of Belief

There is a wide spectrum of belief and practice within Islam, just as there is within Christianity. Yet most Muslims, like most Christians, derive their beliefs from a few central sources of authority. For Christians, the Scriptures are the central authority—the Bible, including the Law and the Prophets, the Gospels and the Epistles. For Muslims, the Qur'an is the central authority, along with the *ahadith,* or "stories" about Muhammad. Many Christians consider the teachings and traditions of the church to be highly authoritative also. Just as Christians have these doctrines and practices handed down through the centuries, Muslims rely also on the *ijma'*, or "consensus" of Muslim community, and *qiyas*, or "analogous" interpretations based on the Qur'an. Both religions have a mixture of other sources of truth at the popular level, including preachers, saints, spiritual forces, and dreams or visions.

In the next two chapters, we'll dig deeper into the Five Pillars of Islam, followed by a few Muslim beliefs and a few Christian doctrines, to identify the major sources of disagreement between us. Once we know what separates us, we'll have a better idea where and how to construct a bridge of understanding to our Muslim friends.

4

THE FIVE PILLARS
OF ISLAM

—

Building a bridge of understanding with other people includes learning about their practices and beliefs. We must do the same for our Muslim neighbors. In this chapter we will turn our attention to the practices of Islam, and in the next we will carefully look at the basic beliefs.

Traditional Islamic thought divides the world into two parts: the "house of submission" (*dar al-Islam*), which is composed of regions that are under the structure and order of Islamic authority and governance, and the "abode of war" (*dar al-harb*), which is the natural state of people who do not submit to God and who thus do not accept the order and structure that comes with that submission. Within this system of thought, the house of submission to God, also called the house of peace, is constructed on certain pillars, all of which are expressions of that communal order and structure. Though the number of pillars may differ from one Islamic tradition to another, there are five core pillars recognized by most Muslim communities.

For Christians, a helpful way to understand the importance of the Five Pillars is to consider the two basic approaches people have to sound religious faith: they can approach faith as a matter of sound thinking (orthodoxy) or as a matter of sound practice (orthopraxy). Christian traditions tend to understand themselves by what they think. The great councils of the Christian church were called to settle Christian beliefs. Christians who chose to conform to the decisions of the councils were viewed as orthodox, or "right thinking," in their faith. Those who found themselves outside the decisions of the councils, such as the Arians, the Nestorians, and the Monophysites, were viewed as heterodox, namely, "different thinking," heretical.

By contrast, Islam functions as a lived tradition, one that places great emphasis on people "doing the right things" (orthopraxy) in their day-to-day lives. Most of the world's Muslims, as we have already discussed, identify themselves as people who follow the *sunna* (example) of the acts of the prophet Muhammad that we read about in the *ahadith*. People engage in those acts to gain merit before God. On the day of judgment, God will weigh the good deeds of people against their evil deeds. Those people whose good deeds outweigh their evil deeds will enter paradise, and the degree of that merit will determine the level of paradise they can enter. Those people whose evil deeds outweigh their good deeds will go to hell, or perhaps to purgatory. The Five Pillars of Islam are the most important of the deeds, the structure upon which the house of Islam is built, and they are also among the doors to paradise.[1]

Beginning with the first pillar, the *shahada*, we will now examine each of the Five Pillars. Keep in mind that for most Muslims, these pillars define what it means to be Muslim.

Shahada

The first pillar of Islam is the *shahada*, the "witness," or statement of faith. The *shahada* consists of the following words: "There is no God but Allah, and Muhammad is his prophet." To repeat this statement of faith with intention is all that is required to become a Muslim. It is recited in each of the five daily prayer rituals. The *shahada* contains the two basic assertions that distinguish Muslims from other religious traditions surrounding them. "There is no God but Allah" distinguishes followers of Muhammad from the pagan traditions of pre-Islamic Arabia. "And Muhammad is his prophet" separates the Muslim community from Christians and Jews who are monotheistic but do not recognize the authority of Muhammad as the Seal of the Prophets, the final authoritative revelation brought to correct the errors of those prophets who preceded him.[2]

The *shahada* may be whispered by a father into the ear of a newborn or by a loved one into the ear of someone about to pass from this life. In many Sufi rituals, the phrase serves as a mantra that is repeated over and over until the practitioner reaches a trancelike state. It appears on the flags of nations and is inscribed on the sides of buildings. By extension, one who dies in the performance of a religious duty, or perhaps even one who dies a patriotic death defending one's country, is generally viewed as a *shaheed*, or "one who bears witness" to Islam.

For those in evangelical Christian traditions, repeating the *shahada* has a similar significance to confessing Jesus Christ as one's Lord and Savior.

Salat

Five times a day Muslims affirm the primary pillar of Islam in a second pillar, the ritual of *salat*, or "prayer." The obligatory times for prayer are before dawn, at noon, in late afternoon, at sunset, and after dark. Islamic prayers are normally a communal rather than an individual event. The *muezzin* (caller) issues a call to prayer, usually broadcast from the minaret of the mosque. Worshippers then prepare for prayers by removing their sandals and by washing their hands and face with water or, if water is not available, with sand. If they are at the mosque, they then line up in the prayer line, marked by carpet on the floor. If people are away from the mosque, a mat is laid out on the floor or ground, if it is available. People then prostrate and rise from the mat a fixed numbers of times, repeating a prayer that declares the greatness of God and the lowliness of humanity before him. After obligatory prayers have been completed, people may continue to pray to offer individual supplications or petitions known as *du'a*.

Women usually conduct prayers in a separate location.[3]

The rhythm of the day in devout communities is marked by the collective trip to the mosque to pray. The exact time when each prayer session is scheduled is dependent upon the time of sunrise and sunset. At times of the year when the sun rises later and sets earlier, the prayers are closer together, and at those times when the sun rises earlier and sets later, the prayers are farther apart.

If this seems unusual or a waste of time in contemporary Western societies, we may want to consider that the lives of Orthodox Christians in traditional communities are often punctuated by similar rituals. In the many communities around the globe where traditional Christians and Muslims live alongside each other, the calls to prayer between the mosque and the church may sound almost antiphonal.

The *qibla*, or direction in which one prays, is important in Islamic tradition. In the early days of Islam, Muhammad commanded his followers to pray toward Jerusalem, following the practice of the Jews of that era. However, during his political leadership of the city of Medina, when he found that the Jews were not accepting his rule, he ordered his followers to turn their backs on Jerusalem, and by extension on those who failed to acknowledge his prophetic role, and to pray in the opposite direction, toward the city of Mecca. From that time forward, Mecca, the city of the pagan pre-Islamic pilgrimage, has been the direction of prayer for all of Islamic tradition. Devout Muslims will carry a compass or an electronic directional device to ensure that the direction of their prayers is correct while traveling.[4] The layout of a mosque is also determined by the *qibla*. When one enters a mosque, the focal point is a niche in the wall, the *mihrab*, that indicates the direction of Mecca. The podium for the preacher is positioned just in front of the *mihrab*, and the floor is covered with square sections of carpet that are seamed together to enable congregants to line up for daily prayers.

There is virtue to conducting prayers in the mosque. But the obligation to public prayers is especially important at noon on Friday and on festival days, when many Muslims will make an effort to pray at a *jami'* mosque, a major community mosque for assembly and prayers.[5] On Friday noon, the prayers are followed by a *khutba*, or sermon, which follows the form of praise to God. Next come blessings upon the Prophet; a moral homily, usually relating to public affairs; and, finally, an invocation of blessing upon the ruler. The person acknowledged in public prayers on Friday is the person recognized as the legitimate political ruler by the community.

If you are visiting a mosque with Muslim friends,[6] you may, quite appropriately, kneel in the back of the room and reverently pray with and for your Muslim friends. However, a male guest should exercise caution to ensure he is not sitting behind women engaged in prayers. If you have devout Muslim friends visiting your home, offer those friends a private room for them to pray at the appointed times. Note: Joining the prayer line with Muslim friends is never appropriate, since the assumption is that if a person has entered the prayer line, he or she has converted to Islam. Praying in the prayer line without having converted to Islam is invariably considered deceptive behavior and would be seriously offensive to many Muslims.

Zakat

A natural extension of worship is charitable giving, or *zakat*, a third pillar of the house of Islam. In its simplest expression, the *zakat* is given for the care of the needy and those indebted, the freeing of slaves, and hospitality toward strangers and wayfarers. Each year, every Muslim of means is expected to pay a percentage of their net worth as a charitable tax for the poor. In its most simple form, such money is given through mosques or other charitable organizations, or it may be given directly to people who are known to be poor.

While Christians historically give of their revenues each year, theoretically Muslims are expected to calculate the value of all of their assets and to make a contribution of 2.5 percent of their net worth each year. Just as certain European countries collect church taxes from their residents, the *zakat* is a mandatory tax collected by the government in countries such as Saudi Arabia, Pakistan, Sudan, Malaysia, and Yemen. In most Islamic cultures, however, payment of the *zakat* is voluntary.[7]

The *zakat* tax applies to Muslims only. However, prior to the twentieth century, the Islamic world traditionally imposed a *jizya* tax upon Christians in its place as a guarantee of their status as protected peoples and in addition to other land and produce taxes.[8] The *jizya* tax was generally considered to be double the *zakat* tax, or 5 percent of net worth. Groups such as ISIS have attempted to reimpose the *jizya* in contemporary times. Merchants who were from non-Islamic lands, and who were not considered protected peoples among the Muslims, were traditionally expected to pay a 10 percent tax rate on all of their merchandise upon entry or departure from the country. Forms of this tax continue in many localities today.[9]

Sawm

A fourth pillar of Islam is the *sawm*, or the annual fast. Except for those who are physically weak or of unsound mind, those who are engaged in heavy labor or battle, and those who are traveling, all Muslims above ten years of age are expected to fast throughout the month of Ramadan. Islamic fasts differ from most Christian fasts in several ways. First, an Islamic fast begins at dawn and stops at dusk on each of the thirty days of Ramadan, whereas Christians may fast from all but water nonstop for multiple days. Second, the *sawm* involves refraining from all foods and liquids, from smoking cigarettes, and from sexual intercourse, whereas Christians may engage in a partial fast. Finally, the fast of Ramadan is communal and obligatory. Though this is similar to a Catholic or an Orthodox fast, for many Christians, fasting is individual and voluntary.

By tradition, Muslims begin the fast from the first sighting of the moon at dawn of the beginning of the month of Ramadan in a particular region. Because clouds may obscure the moon, the date has historically fluctuated. When the new moon is sighted, youths pass through the community beating drums to awaken residents to prepare for the fast. However, many countries now fix the dates for Ramadan through scientific calculation rather than by physical sighting. Throughout Ramadan, people will awaken early to eat their morning meal before dawn prayers. For the entire day people collectively refrain from eating. When dusk comes, people gather for community meals, breaking the fast together after the evening prayers.

The Ramadan fast is a practice that you might choose to observe, even for a day, with Muslim friends. The breaking of the fast in the evening provides a wonderful opportunity for socializing and the exchange of food. Do not be too time conscious if you plan to participate. If you prepare food for the event, using *halal* meat is a basic courtesy. You can purchase *halal* meat from a local supermarket; it is usually found near the kosher section of the store. If your friends are highly observant, they may also refrain from a range of other products that contain trace elements of foodstuffs that are forbidden in Islam. Asking your friends for guidance in preparing food is wise. Again, if these practices seem strange to us, we must keep in mind that traditional Christian communities often have their own distinct food regulations and rituals for slaughtering animals.

The Ramadan fast is often a challenging time for people who have recently converted from Islam to Christianity, since breaking with that tradition publicly sets them apart from their families and communities. For these new Christians, Ramadan and other such traditions, which they now associate with dead law that is powerless to save, stand in stark contrast to their newfound freedom in Christ through the life-giving Spirit.

—

The Islamic Calendar

The Islamic calendar follows the traditional calendar of the Arab nomads, which was a lunar calendar that lacked established methods for remaining synchronized with the solar calendar. Since twelve lunar months are approximately ten days shorter than a solar year, a calendar based upon twelve lunar months finds that annual events move backward by ten days each year on a solar calendar. Orthodox traditions following the Alexandrian calendar, which is partly based on the lunar calendar, solve this problem through what is called intercalation. They add a thirteenth month of five to six days each year in order to keep in cycle with solar calendars.[10]

However, according to early Islamic tradition, the Prophet received a revelation that Muslims should not follow the Christian practice of intercalation. As a result, Islamic festivals such as Ramadan slowly shift each year in relation to the seasons of the year. Every year, the festival falls approximately ten days earlier on the solar calendar than it fell in the previous year. Because the Islamic calendar, when compared to the Western calendar, loses approximately ten days each year, it, accordingly, loses approximately three years each century.

—

Hajj

A fifth pillar of Islam is the *hajj*, the annual communal pilgrimage to Mecca. Every able-bodied Muslim is expected to take part in the pilgrimage at least once in a lifetime, provided he or she is financially capable.

Historically, the *hajj* has been a great spiritual adventure for devout Muslims from all over the world. For people from the fringes of the Islamic world, such as present-day Indonesia, Mali, or Senegal, it was a saga that required months or years of people's lives and a great financial commitment. Accomplishing the feat required a combination of great land or sea voyages to reach the Arabian Peninsula. Pilgrims would gather at all points of the compass, in Djibouti, in Port Sudan, in Cairo, in Damascus, in south Iraq, and in Arabian ports, to join the great caravans and brave the heat of the Arabian Peninsula in order to complete the *hajj*. Caravans were only a partial protection against the threat of nomads who frequently attacked pilgrim convoys in the last stages of the journey.

Just before arriving in Mecca, pilgrims don white attire. As they enter Mecca, pilgrims visit the well of Zamzam, said to have sustained Hagar and Ishmael, then visit historic sites associated with the school of Islamic law with which their community is affiliated. The central event of the pilgrimage is entering the grand *haram,* or "sacred area," that houses the *Ka'aba* stone and to kiss that great black rock one time while circumambulating the compound seven times as part of a great sea of humanity. After casting stones at a pillar symbolizing the devil, an animal is sacrificed, then people remove their sacred attire, and the official pilgrimage has ended.

Once pilgrims have returned home from the *hajj,* a large party is usually thrown for the participants. Often, pilgrims receive an elevated status for the remainder of their lives in their home communities. Muslims who have been on the pilgrimage to Mecca are awarded the title *hajji* for men and *hajjia* for women, and these titles may largely replace their names for the rest of their lives.

Across history, the *hajj* has remained one of the central unifying events of Islamic culture. The reward for the *hajj* is not only the spiritual accomplishment of the *hajj* but also the cultural experience of meeting and trading with Muslims from around the world. The contemporary pilgrimage to Mecca is the largest single gathering on the planet each year. The Saudi government and religious establishment, who are the guardians of the *hajj* today, undertake an extraordinary annual logistical enterprise to guarantee that millions of pilgrims from around the world have an opportunity to participate safely.

There are many parallels between the *hajj* and traditional pilgrimages to Jerusalem. Historically, both events have involved tremendous sacrifice and an investment of months on the part of the faithful. Arab nomadic tribes have harassed both types of pilgrims. People feel they are greatly benefited spiritually from these pilgrimages. Today, both pilgrimages are most frequently done by high-speed travel. This has had a revolutionary effect on the number of people who participate even as it has changed the spiritual importance of these events. However, for Christians, the pilgrimage to Jerusalem is almost entirely voluntary, while for Muslims, the journey to Mecca is expected of all who can participate. To understand the profound meaning of the *hajj* for Muslims, one has only to consider the life-changing impact many Christians feel from a journey to the Holy Land. A sense of sacredness imbues the places we know and have experienced in the reading of Scripture.

In "high" Islamic culture, the *hajj* to Mecca is the only pilgrimage that is required of Muslims, and other pilgrimages may by looked upon as *bid'a*, or (syncretistic) "innovation," on the part of those who advocate them. However, traditional Islamic communities around the world have long been drawn to local holy sites from which the faithful believe great power may be derived. These local holy sites are found in almost every Islamic culture. Wahhabi puritan missionaries from Saudi Arabia have strongly discouraged such practices, and that has affected the popularity of such pilgrimages. But in many areas of the Islamic world, such local pilgrimages retain great spiritual significance in the lives of pious Muslims.

How do we make sense of the Five Pillars of Islam as Christians? Readers raised in a conservative tradition might have some sympathy for a worldview built on right practices. To be a part of conservative Christianity has traditionally meant doing some things and not doing others. Observing the Sabbath, tithing, and attending worship gatherings are among the required practices. They go hand in hand with the avoidance of other practices, such as drinking alcohol, gambling, and illicit sexual behavior. Many of these dos and don'ts remain cornerstones of communal identity and of Christian virtue within the community.

Now that we have finished our introduction to the Five Pillars—the practices of Islam—let us turn our attention to what Muslims believe and explore how those beliefs separate Muslims from Christians.

5
WHAT SEPARATES US

—

Our aim is to build a bridge of understanding to our Muslim neighbors so we can break the chain of ignorance and hatred, replacing it with understanding, respect, and love. To do that, we must frankly admit that there is indeed a gulf separating Muslims and Christians. As we've already seen, the history of Christian and Muslim interactions has, on occasion, been marred by unfortunate events and difficulties. We do not understand each other very well, and that misunderstanding often leads to prejudice and suspicion. Also, there are significant differences in our beliefs. While we do have much in common, as we will see in the following chapters, there are at least four fundamental differences between these two faiths. They are seen in our respective answers to these questions:

• Who is God?
• Who is Jesus?
• Are the Scriptures reliable?
• What is the remedy for sin?

Let's explore each of these, noting both what we have in common and where we differ. When we are finished, you'll have a much better understanding of the Muslim faith, and possibly of your own. And you will gain confidence for talking with your Muslim neighbors on matters of faith.

Who Is God?

Who is God? The answer to that question creates the first chasm of difference between Christians and Muslims. Christianity and Islam, also Judaism, are monotheistic faiths. They all hold that there is one true God. But are they speaking about the same God? What is this God like? Can he be known? How does he relate to humankind? Timothy George has summed up the question we are asking in his intriguing book title, *Is the Father of Jesus the God of Muhammad?*[1] To answer that question, we will look at two key concepts: God's attributes and God's name.

God's Attributes

Both Muslim and Christian theologians write much about the attributes or characteristics of God. They are trying to answer the question, "What is God like?" Let's answer that question both from a Muslim and Christian point of view, beginning with what we both believe about the character of God.

What We Both Believe. The Christian and Muslim views of God have a lot in common. Both faiths affirm the following statements:

- God is one.
- God is holy.
- God is eternal.
- God is perfect—there is nothing lacking in him.
- God is the creator and sustainer of all.
- God is merciful.
- God is just.
- God is all-knowing.
- God is all-powerful.
- God is present everywhere.
- God is high and lifted up (transcendent).
- God has a will for all humankind.

Where We Disagree. Muslims and Christians share many common understandings of God. However, there are also some important differences.

1. *God's most dominant characteristic.*[2] If Muslims were forced to pick the one characteristic of God that is most significant, it would likely be the *will* of God. God has a divine will, and it is the duty of humanity to submit to that will. The primary Muslim message is, "Submit to the will of God." If Christians were forced to pick the one most significant characteristic of God, it would probably be the *love* of God. The primary Christian message is, "God loves you."

To Muslims, it is unimportant (and probably unknowable) whether or not God loves you. The important thing to know is God's will for you. The Sufis reacted against this rather austere picture of God, and Sufi literature is replete with discussions of God's love. However, that represents a minority way of thinking within Islam.

2. *God's immanence.* Both Muslims and Christians accept the transcendence of God. Isaiah's vision of God as "high and lifted up" (Isa. 6:1, KJV) is a good depiction of this. But for Christians, the counterbalance to the transcendence of God is his immanence, or nearness. God dwells within each person through the Holy Spirit. Isaiah captures both ideas in 57:15: "For this is what the high and exalted One says—he who lives forever, whose name is holy: 'I live in a high and holy place, but also with the one who is contrite and lowly in spirit'" (NIV). The apostle Paul writes to the Corinthians, "Don't you know that you yourselves are God's temple and that God's Spirit dwells in your midst?" (1 Cor. 3:16, NIV).

That concept is simply not prominent in traditional Islam. God is exalted and distant, not personally involved with individuals. Again the Sufis are an exception to this view, stressing that God is nearby to the believer. Their view is derived from a single verse in the Qur'an: "We have created man, and We know what his own-self whispers to him. And We are nearer to him than his jugular vein" (Qur'an 50:16, al-Hilali).

3. *The triune nature of God.* This is the widest chasm between the two faiths—a nonnegotiable point on both sides. Christians categorically uphold the concept of the Trinity, that God is one being who exists in three persons: Father, Son, and Spirit. Muslims emphatically deny that idea. Muslims often mistakenly believe that the Trinity comprises God the Father, Mary, and their offspring, Jesus, an idea perhaps derived from exposure to folk orthodox traditions in Muhammad's own time. Muslims find this idea repugnant, and of course, Christians do as well.

Muhammad's primary message was arguably the unicity of God (*tawhid*). God alone is God, and no person or thing can be made to be equal with him. To do such is to commit the greatest of all sins, *shirk.* Therefore, Christians commit this grave sin of *shirk* when they associate Jesus with God. Interestingly, while Christians commit *shirk* by equating Jesus with God, Muslims claim that the Qur'an, in the form of the Heavenly Tablet, coexisted with God from all time, yet they do not consider this to be committing *shirk.* So associating the written Word (Qur'an) with God is not *shirk*, but associating the Living Word (Jesus) with God is considered *shirk.* This anomaly can serve as a bridge of communication, for if associating Jesus, the Living Word, with God, is considered *shirk,* then considering the Qur'an to coexist with God must be *shirk* also; but if the latter is not shirk, then, surely, the former is not shirk either.

God's Name

The name used for God is another chasm between Christianity and Islam, but it is a false one. Muslims have claimed that only they can use the name *Allah* because it originated with Muhammad. In Malaysia, for instance, Christians are not allowed to use the word *Allah* to refer to God. However, the name *al-Lah* was already being used in Arabia to designate the highest god when Muhammad arrived on the scene in the seventh century. He appropriated the name to refer to the one God, much as the Israelites appropriated the Canaanite name *El* as a compound in so many biblical names for God, including *El Roi, Elohim,* and *El Shaddai.* The name *Allah* is used by Christians in Muslim lands to refer to God. The term did not originate with Islam.

Do We Worship the Same God?

Let's return to the question with which we started: "Is the Father of Jesus the God of Muhammad?" Yes and no. With respect to the concept of the Trinity, no—they are not the same. Christians know God as Creator, as Savior, and as Indwelling Presence. Christians believe that God is one, existing in three persons: Father, Son, and Holy Spirit. Muslims cannot accept this formulation, so from this standpoint the two understandings of God are very different.

However, from other standpoints, the answer is most definitely yes—God the Father is the God of Muhammad. Muhammad believed the God he proclaimed was the same God worshipped by Jews and Christians, which is why he was so disappointed that they did not rally to his message. In the Pentateuch, God often introduces himself as the God of Abraham, Isaac, and Jacob. If a Muslim were asked to identify his God, he, too, would say that Allah is the God of Abraham, Isaac, and Jacob.

In support of this idea, consider Paul's ministry to the Athenians (see Acts 17). Paul had gone to Mars hill to address the Court of Areopagus. On the way, he noted the various idols the Athenians worshipped. In his address, Paul commented on an idol honoring an "unknown God." He said, "What therefore you worship as unknown, this I proclaim to you" (Acts 17:23, NRSV). Paul could have said, "Oh, you idolatrous Athenians. Your idea of God is absolutely unacceptable. It is so wrong. God is completely different than any of your idols." And had Paul chosen that approach, he might have been theologically correct. But he would not have been effective as an evangelist. Paul chose to build on the Athenians' admittedly flawed understanding of God. In essence he said to them, "You have an incomplete picture of God. I want to tell you more about him."

In the same way, we would not say that the understanding of God held by Muslims is the same as the Christian understanding of God. Yet we can say that they worship the same God, though with an incomplete picture of who he is. Undoubtedly, many Christians also have an incomplete or erroneous conception of who God is. Nevertheless, we acknowledge that we are all seeking to know the same God. We can acknowledge that with Muslims too. In his valuable book *Kissing Cousins?* Bill Musk suggests that "our role as Christians . . . needs to be one of accepting the use of the term *Allah* and seeking to fill that term with biblical meaning."[3] Some things about the Muslim understanding of God are biblically accurate. Others are not compatible with the biblical picture of God. We should affirm and strengthen the former while patiently challenging the latter.

Who Is Jesus?

Five centuries before the birth of Muhammad, the apostle Paul wrote these words: "We preach Christ crucified: a stumbling block to Jews and foolishness to Gentiles" (1 Cor. 1:23, NIV). Had Islam existed when Paul lived, he might have written the verse this way: "We preach Christ crucified: a stumbling block to both Jews and Muslims and foolishness to the Gentiles." Neither Jews nor Muslims accept that Jesus is the Son of God or that his crucifixion is the key element in God's plan of salvation. The Christian view of Jesus is both the centerpiece of our faith and a great chasm between Muslims and us.

What Christians Believe about Jesus

Though we don't know exactly when and how the Apostles' Creed was written, its authority for defining orthodox faith has not been questioned. After affirming belief "in God the Father, Almighty, Maker of heaven and earth," the creed makes a number of clear statements about Jesus Christ. He is God's "only begotten Son, our Lord: Who was conceived by the Holy Ghost, born of the Virgin Mary: Suffered under Pontius Pilate; was crucified, dead and buried: He descended into hell: The third day he rose again from the dead: He ascended into heaven, and sits at the right hand of God the Father Almighty: From thence he shall come to judge the quick and the dead."[4] Virtually every Christian body has affirmed this creed for the last seventeen centuries—possibly longer. This book is not primarily about the Christian view of Christ, so I won't comment further, except to say that the Apostles' Creed (as well as the Nicene Creed) clearly states the Christian view of Jesus as both Son of God and Savior of the world.

What Muslims Believe about Jesus

Muslims have a very high view of Jesus. He is mentioned nearly one hundred times in the Qur'an, variously referred to as Son of Mary, Isa (Jesus), and the Messiah. The Qur'an also credits Jesus with performing many miracles, which validated his status as a prophet. However, there are important differences in how Muslims and Christians see Jesus. Let's look at a few of these.

A Prophet Second to Muhammad. Though Muslims acknowledge that Jesus was a prophet, they see him as secondary to Muhammad. Jesus never married, so cannot be an example of married life. Jesus never ran a city or a country; therefore, he cannot understand the difficulties in doing so. He never won battles as a general, so he never had a chance to show benevolence as conqueror. Muhammad did all of those things and is therefore superior to Jesus.

Miraculous Birth. The Qur'an recounts the miraculous birth of Jesus to the Virgin Mary in Sura 19, appropriately titled "Mary." However, there are significant differences in the Qur'anic version of the story. God's spirit, in the form of a "well-made man" (Qur'an 19:17, Shakir), told her she would give birth to a "pure boy" (Qur'an 19:19, Shakir). It is believed that Gabriel breathed into her and she became pregnant. When the time for the birth came, Mary withdrew to a secluded place and sat by the trunk of a palm tree. While she was in the throes of labor, God provided a stream for water and told her to shake the tree so ripe dates would fall for her to eat. When she returned to her people, they accused her of being unchaste, but Jesus spoke from the cradle to defend her (Qur'an 19:1–32). Jesus was born sinless because he was protected from Satan's touch by Gabriel.

Half of the Qur'anic verses mentioning Jesus deal with his birth. Four passages mention his death, and two of these treat it as a normal death. The third is unclear, and the fourth appears to categorically deny that Jesus died by crucifixion. This emphasis is quite different from the Gospels, where Jesus's death is detailed at great length and only two writers even mention his birth.

Unique, but Not Divine. Two unique appellations are accorded to Jesus by Muslims. A Christian would look at these names and see big arrows pointing to Jesus's divinity, but Muslims do not interpret them that way. First, Jesus is repeatedly called the *Messiah,* a label unique to him in Islam. But what does this term mean? Fakhr al-Din al-Razi, a twelfth-century Persian theologian, offered several explanations for the title *Messiah.* Possibly it meant not that Jesus was anointed but that he anointed others—such as the sick and orphans. Or perhaps Jesus was the anointed one, but that means only that he was born sinless or was anointed with oil or was brushed by Gabriel's wing. Though the title is meant as praise for Jesus, it does not indicate his divinity.[5]

The second unique name for Christ in Islam is *Word of God*.[6] In Sura 4:171, we read, "Christ Jesus the son of Mary was (no more than) an apostle of Allah, and His Word, which He bestowed on Mary, and a spirit proceeding from Him" (Yusuf Ali). Is Jesus called this because of his miraculous birth? If so, we would expect Adam to have the same title, for his birth was miraculous also. Or is it because Jesus preached God's Word with great boldness? If so, why is Muhammad not called this also? *Word of God* is a most intriguing appellation for Jesus, and Muslims are content to let this go unexplored.

A Man, Not God. When Christians refer to Jesus as the Son of God, we do not mean a biological son but rather that he is in very nature God. There is a curious verse in the Qur'an that deals with this concept: "Say, 'If (Allah) Most Gracious had a son, I would be the first to worship'" (Qur'an 43:81, Yusuf Ali). There are five usual interpretations of this verse ranging from an affirmation that Allah could not possibly have had a son to a conditional statement that shows Muhammad's submission to God (even if he *did* have a son, I would still worship Allah). Muslims do not interpret this verse to mean that Jesus is the Son of God or that such a relationship is possible. Thus, even though Jesus is given divine names, and there are verses that at least open the door to his divinity, Muslims categorically refute this idea. Jesus was only a man.

Ministry Limited to the Jews. Christians believe that Jesus came for the whole world (John 3:16) and that he sent his disciples out to reach the whole world (Matt. 28:19–20). Muslims disagree. They point to Muhammad as the prophet for the whole world, believing Jesus was the Messiah of the Jews only. This view is based on two passages in the Gospel of Matthew. One is where Jesus said to the Canaanite woman, "I was sent only to the lost sheep of Israel" (15:24, NIV). The second is the commissioning of the Twelve, when Jesus said, "Do not go among the Gentiles or enter any town of the Samaritans. Go rather to the lost sheep of Israel" (10:5–6, NIV).

Did Not Die on the Cross. The crucifixion, death, burial, and resurrection of Jesus are foundational for all Christian belief. In writing to the Corinthians, Paul talks about the centrality of this issue to our faith. "If there is no resurrection of the dead, then not even Christ has been raised. And if Christ has not been raised, our preaching is useless. . . . Your faith is futile; you are still in your sins. . . . We are of all people most to be pitied" (1 Cor. 15:13–14, 17, 19, NIV).

Yet Muslims are adamant that Jesus did not die on the cross. Since they reject any necessity of atonement (as we'll see in a moment), they see the saving death of Jesus as unnecessary. And there is no possibility that an omnipotent God would allow one of his prophets to die in this way. Muslims believe that God intervened, either by providing a substitute who looked like Jesus to die in his place or by causing him to faint on the cross so that the disciples could remove him and put him in the cool cave where he revived.

The crucifixion is a focal point that clarifies the contrasting beliefs of Judaism, Islam, and Christianity. The Jews say that Jesus was not sent by God, which is why he was crucified. Muslims say that Jesus was sent by God, which is why he was not crucified. Christians say that Jesus was sent by God and was crucified nevertheless.[7] The chasm between Muslims and Christians is perhaps widest here, on the question of Jesus's identity. To Christians, Jesus is the Son of God, the Savior of the world. To Muslims, Jesus is a great prophet, but just a man who was sent to minister to the Jewish people.

Are the Scriptures Reliable?

The issue here is whether the Qur'an and the Bible are the inspired Word of God and can be trusted to guide the followers of each faith. Not surprisingly, this question is answered differently by adherents of each religion.

What Christians Believe about the Scriptures

The Christian view of the Bible is that it is the inspired Word of God. Though Christians may hold differing opinions on the concept of biblical inerrancy and on principles of biblical interpretation, there is general agreement that the Bible, both Old and New Testaments, is inspired by God and is a reliable, authoritative guide for faith and life.

Christians do not accept that the Qur'an is the inspired Word of God. Beyond that, Christians (and others) who have read the Qur'an usually find it difficult to read with understanding. Though it contains some nuggets of truth, these are deeply buried in what seem to be confusing and meandering verses. Some of the problems Christians find with the Qur'an include the following: the meanings of many words are unclear, some passages reference ideas or events that can't be positively identified, there appear to be insertions and revisions in the text, there are grammatical errors in the original Arabic, and some phrases, sentences, and verses don't fit their context and seem to have been transposed.[8]

What Muslims Believe about the Scriptures

Muslims believe the Qur'an is the word of God, given to the prophet Muhammad by the angel Gabriel. Because they believe in a mechanical view of transmission—that the Qur'an was literally dictated to Muhammad, who memorized it, then recited it to his followers, who recorded it—the Qur'an is completely reliable.

They believe it to be a unique, inimitable book that has existed eternally. It is the highest authority in Islam.

Muslim positions on the Bible are much more complicated. Muslims accept that God did inspire parts of the Jewish and Christian Scriptures, specifically the Pentateuch, Psalms, and Gospels. However, they do not accept the reliability of these writings in their current form.

Corruptions to the Bible. Muslims believe the Scriptures have been corrupted by the very people to whom they were given and are therefore unreliable. Muslims feel there are numerous places where Christians or Jews either added or subtracted words from the text, substituted words, or purposely concealed the true meaning of a verse or word. This is the Muslim explanation for the discrepancies between the Qur'an and the Bible on certain events such as the birth of Jesus.

The Bible Foretells Muhammad. According to Muslims, the most serious corruption of the Bible is that both Jews and Christians removed biblical references foretelling the coming of Muhammad. Two passages draw particular attention on this point. The first is Deuteronomy 18:18, where Moses recounts what God had said to him. "I will raise up for them [the Israelites] a prophet like you [Moses] from among their fellow Israelites, and I will put my words in his mouth. He will tell them everything I command him" (NIV).

Muslims believe this coming prophet is none other than Muhammad. Because Muhammad was a descendant of Ishmael, he was a brother to the Israelites, who are descendants of Isaac. Also, Muhammad has much more in common with Moses than did Jesus and was more "like" Moses than was Jesus. Finally, the last part of the verse seems to support the idea that through this prophet God would faithfully tell the people everything that God had dictated to him—a possible reference to the Qur'an.

Christians, of course, believe this verse looks forward to Jesus, who was a true descendant from among the Israelites. Of Abraham's children, only Isaac is referred to as the son of promise. And Jesus himself accepts that Moses spoke about him, saying, "If you believed Moses, you would believe me, for he wrote about me" (John 5:46, NIV).[9]

A second biblical passage thought to refer to Muhammad is Jesus's teaching on the Comforter in John 14–16. The Greek word for comforter is *paraklētos* and is similar to the Greek word for famed or praised, which is *periklytos*. Muslims claim that the original Scripture had the second word, *periklytos,* not the first word, *paraklētos.* The Arabic term for "praised" can be *Ahmad.* This is similar to *Ahamad*, a variant spelling of *Muhammad.*[10] Christians understand that when Jesus spoke of the Comforter who was to come after him, he referred to the Holy Spirit.

What Is the Remedy for Sin?

Christians and Muslims agree that the first people to sin were Adam and Eve. However, that is the extent of their agreement on the subject. The two faiths disagree about the root cause of sin and, therefore, the remedy for it.

What Christians Believe about Sin

Christians believe that first Eve and then Adam sinned by willfully and knowingly disobeying God's command not to eat the forbidden fruit. As a result of their action, "sin entered the world through one man, and death through sin, and in this way death came to all people, because all sinned. . . . Consequently, just as one trespass resulted in condemnation for all people . . . through the disobedience of the one man the many were made sinners" (Rom. 5:12, 18–19, NIV). So sin was both their act of disobedience *and* the state of condemnation that has been inherited by all future generations. We call this *original sin*.

Original sin is the corruption of human nature, shared by all offspring of Adam. We are born in a state of rebellion from God and have an innate inclination to do evil.[11] Sin is also the individual acts of wronging that all people inevitably commit. Sin is a voluntary violation of a known law of God by a morally responsible person. It is, therefore, not to be confused with involuntary and inescapable shortcomings, infirmities, faults, mistakes, failures, or other unintended deviations from God's perfect standard. So because Adam and Eve purposefully sinned, all people have inherited the effects of that sin. Because of this, all people commit sins (Rom. 3:23), and the "wages of sin is death" (6:23, NIV).

If defiance of God is the problem, what is the solution? Salvation from sin comes only through Jesus Christ (Acts 4:12). No one can save himself by his own good works (Eph. 2:8–9). God graciously gives us salvation from sin through faith in his Son, Jesus Christ. For our dire predicament, God provided a costly remedy. He sent Jesus, who was never corrupted by original sin—and who never committed a sin—to live on earth for a time, then die on the cross as the perfect sacrifice for our wrongdoing. Because Christ died for us, we need not be punished for our sins. God thus reaches out to all people and by his grace enables everyone to choose whether or not to accept his saving gift.[12] When we accept Jesus through faith—that is, when we believe in him (John 1:12)—God grants us a new and eternal life.

What Muslims Believe about Sin

Muslims believe that Adam and Eve did sin, but that it was not done in rebellion against God but by mistake. They were full of enthusiasm to do good and thought they *were* doing so. They were wrong, and when they realized their error, they repented. God forgave them, and that was the end of it. There were no permanent results from this initial sin. In other words, there is no such thing as original sin in Islam. Instead, Muslims believe that every child is born in a state of purity called *fitra* and is naturally inclined to do good.

So if there is no original sin, what accounts for the fact that all people sin? They sin because they are forgetful. People keep forgetting God's commands, which is why God has sent some 124,000 prophets to remind them. This also explains why, in Muslim lands, mosques and minarets dot the landscape, reminding people to pray five times a day.

Because Muslims view the sin problem as forgetfulness rather than rebellion, the remedy is mindfulness rather than atonement. Muslims have no need of a savior. Each person is responsible for his or her own predicament. No one else can help the person, and the person has the capability to effect his or her own salvation by submitting to God's commands.

In short, Muslims believe that salvation is earned by submitting to God's will. They picture God as the great judge, holding a scale to measure each person's life. When the person dies, God collects all his or her good works and places them on one side of the scale and places the bad deeds on the other side. The balance determines the eternal destiny of the soul.

Mending Fences

The four main chasms that separate Muslims and Christians may also be thought of as fences or boundaries. These chasms represent the most important beliefs for proponents of each religion—the nonnegotiable boundaries that define us. And boundaries are important. The writer of Proverbs says, "Do not move an ancient boundary stone or encroach on the fields of the fatherless" (23:10, NIV). And the prophet Hosea chastised the leaders of Israel because they moved the ancient boundary stones (5:10). It is important to know who we are and to maintain our identity. We are grateful for the "fences" that define our faith.

However, it is easy for the fences that identify us to become walls of hostility that separate us. The Jews and Samaritans did this in Bible times, and Jews and Arabs have done so in the Middle East. Blacks and whites have built walls of hostility in America, just as the Serbs and Croats have done in the Balkans, and Catholics and Protestants in Ireland. It is important that we not let our boundary fences become walls of prejudice, suspicion, fear, and hatred. In speaking about the Jews and the Gentiles, Paul wrote that Christ Jesus had brought the two together and "has destroyed the barrier, the dividing wall of hostility" (Eph. 2:14, NIV). That was true two thousand years ago for Jews and Gentiles, and it is true today for Christians and Muslims. In the next section of this book, we'll begin to see how we might mend these fences, or bridge the chasms that have separated us from our Muslim neighbors.

Part II
Materials for Bridge Building

6
PIERS OF COMMONALITY
—

A pier is a vertical column that supports a portion of the span of a bridge. Piers have to be strong and well grounded because the weight of the bridge must rest on them. If we are to build a bridge of understanding with our Muslim neighbors, we must identify strong points of commonality between us. We need some piers on which to build our bridge. The chasm is indeed wide, so we'll need to have firm supports that can be a basis for communication and discovery.

In this chapter, we'll identify points of general commonality between Muslims and Christians. These are not points of absolute agreement, but they do provide shared history or beliefs or other similarities. In the following chapters, we will identify three more specific points that we have in common. For now, we are looking at broad areas of commonality.

Remember that these piers, or points of commonality, exist within a chasm. So while both Muslims and Christians both talk about sin (a commonality), they begin with different conceptions of what sin is (a chasm). That being said, these piers of commonality are a good place to initiate dialogue while remembering that we may both use the same term with slightly different meanings. Four piers of general commonality might be suggested:

- Historical Commonalities
- Scriptural Commonalities
- Theological Commonalities
- Missional Commonalities

Historical Commonalities

Jews, Christians, and Muslims all legitimately claim Abraham as their father. Jews and Christians trace their lineage through Abraham and Sarah and their son, Isaac, whereas Muslims trace theirs through Abraham and Hagar and their son, Ishmael. Muhammad was genuinely disappointed and, frankly, confused that the Jews of Mecca and Medina did not immediately sense a kinship with him and join his new movement. He felt that the piers of commonality were so strong and obvious that they would immediately see them and accept him. In the beginning, he taught his followers that the *qibla* (the direction to face when praying) pointed toward Jerusalem. But when he finally realized the Jews would not follow him, he changed the *qibla* from Jerusalem to Mecca.

When dialoging with our Muslim neighbors, we can rightly sense and appeal to our common ancestry through Abraham. For Christians and for many Muslims, this is a spiritual ancestry and not a biological one. We are not literal children of Abraham but are his offspring in faith.

Scriptural Commonalities

Judaism, Christianity, and Islam each point to a divinely inspired Scripture text. In fact, it is largely the same text. *Old Testament* is the Christian term for the Jewish Scriptures. When Jesus said, "Do not think that I have come to abolish the Law or the Prophets; I have not come to abolish them but to fulfill them" (Matt. 5:17, NIV), he confirmed the Jewish Scriptures as part of the canon of Christianity. To those thirty-nine books, Christians added the twenty-seven books of the New Testament. These are the sixty-six books that we call the Christian Scriptures. Christians have always accepted the Old Testament as the divinely inspired Word of God, a true pier of commonality between Jews and Christians.

Six hundred years later, the Qur'an referred to Jews and Christians as "people of the book" and spoke very highly of the Bible. The Bible is referred to, among other terms, as the "Book of God," the "Word of God," a "light and guidance to man," a "decision for all matters," a "guidance and mercy," the "lucid Book," the "illumination (al-furqan)," and a "guidance and warning to those who fear God."[1] Muslims accept a portion of both the Jewish and Christian Scriptures as divinely inspired: the Torah, the Psalms, and the Gospels. At one point, the Qur'an refers Muhammad back to previous revelations given to the Jews and the Christians to confirm the truth of what was being revealed to him: "So if you (O Muhammad) are in doubt concerning that which We have revealed unto you, [i.e. that your name is written in the Taurat (Torah) and the Injeel (Gospel)] then ask those who are reading the Book [the Taurat (Torah) and the Injeel (Gospel)] before you. Verily, the truth has come to you from your Lord. So be not of those who doubt (it)" (Qur'an 10:94, al-Hilali). Scripture is a very strong pier of commonality between Christians and Muslims.

Yet despite these affirmations of the Bible within the Qur'an, this pier is weakened because Muhammad and the Qur'an separate themselves from the Bible, claiming it has been corrupted. When dialoguing with our Muslim neighbors, we can build on the pier of Scripture but must do so carefully. It is important not to disparage the Qur'an or debate the veracity of the Bible but rather to build upon the many points that they have in common.

Theological Commonalities

Though there are significant differences in the beliefs of Christians and Muslims, there are also significant commonalities. Theological commonalities form a third pier on which our bridge of understanding may be built.

Monotheism

The unicity of God is perhaps the strongest doctrine presented in the Qur'an. Nothing can be paired to God; to do so is to engage in the sin of *shirk*, one of the gravest sins that a Muslim can commit. Christians, too, are monotheistic, despite the Muslim claim that Christians worship three gods. This is another example of a general pier of commonality that can be found within a chasm of difference.

Character of God

Many of God's characteristics are affirmed by both faiths. Christians and Muslims agree that God is the Creator of all things and that he is greater than his creation. Both believe that God has a will or plan for his creation, and when we follow that plan, we find happiness and joy. Both faiths hold that human beings understand what God wills through his revealed Word and through those feelings of "ought," which Christians commonly label *conscience*.

Human Accountability

Christians and Muslims both believe that human beings are accountable to God for their actions. This is true in an eschatological sense, for there is a final judgment in which all people will face God to be held accountable for their lives. And both faiths hold to a present-day responsibility for humankind, though they present the idea differently. Muslims see human beings as vice-regents for God here on earth, ruling in his place. Christians understand that they are commanded to "subdue" the earth (Gen. 1:28, NASB).

These theological commonalities are a strong pier for building understanding. There are a number of points on which the faiths are in total agreement, and others where our differences are based partly on the misunderstanding of a doctrine, such as the Christian doctrine of the Trinity.

Missional Commonalities

A fourth pier of commonality between Islam and Christianity is the activist bent of both religions. Unlike some other faiths, for example, Judaism, which do not hold adherents responsible for gaining followers and impacting the world, Christianity and Islam share a strong sense of mission.

Missionary Impulse

Christianity and Islam are evangelistic, missionary-oriented religions. The challenge of the Great Commission pushes Christians out to reach those who have not accepted Christ. The challenge of *da'wa* pushes Muslims with equal force to "witness" to those who have not yet chosen the way of *islam* (surrender to God). These faiths are in aggressive competition to win converts, which is often a point of conflict. For example, it is illegal in many Muslim countries to attempt to convert someone from Islam to Christianity. Yet this mission-mindedness is also a pier of commonality. Both Christians and Muslims understand the need and urgency of bringing people to God.

Sense of Urgency

Both faiths have a very strong eschatological viewpoint. Gaining heaven and avoiding hell are prime concerns for Christians and Muslims alike. Here again, however, a pier of commonality rests in a chasm of difference. While both faiths hold to a literal view of heaven and hell and see the latter as a place of constant suffering, Christians and Muslims have a vastly different understanding of the reward awaiting the faithful in heaven. Whereas a Christian often views heaven as a place of eternal worship and praise to God, Islamic descriptions of *jannah* focus more often on the sensual pleasures that are the reward to the believer. Muslims believe there are five levels of heaven, with the highest level restricted to the Prophet and those most deserving of that merit.

Building on the Piers of Commonality

Christians and Muslims have a great deal in common historically, scripturally, theologically, and missionally. These areas form four solid piers on which mutual understanding may be built. Upon this foundation of general commonalities between the two religions, we can lay "planks" of more specific commonality to create our bridge of understanding. These planks are specific doctrines taught both by Islam and by most orthodox Christian bodies. In each of the next three chapters, we will explore these three planks from both the Christian and Muslim points of view. Our three planks of specific commonality are these:

- Intention
- Holiness
- Struggle

Use these chapters to sharpen your understanding of both viewpoints so you can be prepared to talk about them with a Muslim friend.

7
PLANK ONE: INTENTION

—

Having established a foundation for our bridge of understanding, the four piers of commonality through history, Scripture, theology, and mission, it's time to lay some planks on the bridge. These planks are the more specific teachings where we have much more in common. In fact, these planks are ways in which we are more alike than different. They will form an ideal walkway for discussing faith with our Muslim neighbors. The first plank on our bridge of understanding is the concept of *intention*, an idea held in common by Islam and Christianity.

Intention is a determination to act in a certain manner. Synonyms for *intention* include *purpose*, *objective*, and *goal*. Our intentions are the thoughts in our minds that we propose to make reality. Intention is located in a person's inner life. It is an activity of the mind and heart, not of the hands and legs. In spiritual matters, intention is synonymous with motivation. Our physical actions are triggered by our inner thoughts and motivations—our intentions. As Jesus said, "It is out of the abundance of the heart that the mouth speaks" (Luke 6:45, NRSV). This inner aspect of our lives forms the first plank on our bridge of understanding to our Muslim neighbors.

The Muslim Concept of Intention

The Arabic word for intention is *niyya*, an expression very important to Muslims. Prior to daily prayers, Muslims express their intention to perform their prayer obligation toward God. If they do not make this expression of intent, their prayers have no effect. So it is when they perform the fast. They must declare their *niyya*—resolve or intention—to do so prior to undertaking the task. Likewise with the *hajj*, or pilgrimage to Mecca. And when Muslims arrive in Mecca, they cry out "*Labbaika Allahumma Labbaik*," meaning "Here am I, Lord, here am I."[1] Why is this concept so important for Muslims? Let's answer that by turning to their primary sources of authority: the Qur'an and the *ahadith*.

Intention in the Qur'an

Though intention is not a prominent concept in the Qur'an, there is one passage that deals with it very clearly. Sura 37 contains the story of Abraham offering his son on the altar. Acting on a command Abraham feels he has received from God, he lays his son facedown upon the altar and prepares to sacrifice him. Then God calls out to Abraham, "O Abraham: Thou hast already fulfilled the vision. Lo! thus do We reward the good. Lo! that verily was a clear test" (Qur'an 37:104–106, Pickthall). Abraham's hand was stayed. He did not literally kill his son in sacrifice to God. But according to the Qur'an, because he was willing and prepared to do so, God considered *that he had done it*. Abraham's intention to sacrifice his son was seen by God as equivalent to doing it.

Intention in the Ahadith

If the Qur'an says little about the concept of intention, that is more than counterbalanced by the large amount of material in the *ahadith* on this subject. Muslim scholar Ibn Rajab al-Hanbali (1335–92) compiled a collection of fifty key ideas from the *ahadith* in his book titled *The Compendium of Knowledge and Wisdom.* The first chapter is titled "Intention." The two most respected collections of *ahadith,* by Bukhari and Muslim, begin with this same subject. The concept of intention is indeed very important to Muslims.

The keystone *hadith* dealing with intention is attributed to 'Umar bin al-Khattab, the second caliph. "I heard Allah's Apostle saying, 'The reward of deeds depends upon the intentions and every person will get the reward according to what he has intended.'"[2] In other words, it is the person's motivation when performing a deed that gives it validity, not the act itself. The famous eighth-century jurist al-Shafi'i said that this single *hadith* represents one-third of all the knowledge and teachings of Islam. Here are the key ideas for understanding the Muslim concept of intention.

Intentions Matter More than Actions. One brief *hadith* points out that a mediocre act can be made great by good intention and that a great act can be made mediocre by unworthy intention. "Many a small action is exalted by intention, and many a great action is lessened by intention."[3] Another *hadith* explains that on judgment day, intentions will be counted the same as the actual act. "The angel will be called, 'Record so-and-so as such-and-such,' and he will say, 'Lord, he didn't do it!' and He will say, 'He intended it.'"[4]

Good Intentions Outweigh Bad Ones. One *hadith* says that if someone intends to do a good action but does not do it, God will still credit him with doing that good action. However, if he both intends to do the good action and actually does it, God will credit him with ten good actions. On the other hand, if he intends to do wrong but doesn't do it, God makes no marks in his record book. Only bad intentions accompanied by actions are held against a person.[5]

Words, Actions, and Intentions Are Interconnected. One *hadith* in particular is very clear on this point. "Words do not benefit unless there is action, and words and actions do not benefit unless there is action, and words and actions do not benefit unless there are intentions, and words, actions and intentions are no use unless they accord with the *Sunna* [the example of Muhammad]."[6]

Intentions Define Sin. Several *ahadith* show the necessity of having the intent to sin for an action to be considered a sin (versus a mistake or shortcoming). Both Bukhari and Muslim include this *hadith*: "You are not to blame for any honest mistake you make but only for what your hearts premeditate."[7]

Another *hadith* explains the difference between a sin and a mistake. The example given is of a Muslim fighter who intends to kill a *kafir* (unbeliever) but ends up killing a Muslim by mistake.[8] This *hadith* doesn't condemn the killing, because the man did not intend to kill a fellow Muslim. Another *hadith* says that if someone accidently kills an animal or another person, compensatory payment must be made. However, if the action was deliberate, then in addition to compensatory payment, vengeance of some kind is involved.[9]

God's Final Judgment Is Based on Intention. One *hadith* describes three people who face God at the judgment seat following death. The first is a man to whom God has given wisdom. God asks what he has done with his wisdom. "Oh, I have practiced my wisdom day and night."

"You lie," God replies. "All you wanted was for people to notice you and think that you were a great scholar."

The second one has been blessed with great wealth. God asks him what he has done with his wealth. "Oh, I have given out alms day and night."

"You lie," God replies. "All you wanted was for people to notice you and think that you were a great philanthropist."

The third one was a martyr. God asks him why he died as a martyr. "Oh, I followed your command to do *jihad*."

"You lie," God replies. "All you wanted was for people to notice you and think that you were a courageous person."[10] In one version of this story, all three men are dragged on their faces and then thrown into the fire.

It is clear from this *hadith* that the men were rejected by God, not for what they did, but for their motivation in doing it. Their actions were good, but God looked behind their deeds to see the intention of the heart.

Intention as an Act of Worship

Sufism is the branch of Islam that stresses the inner dimension of the Muslim religion, so it is no surprise that much Sufi literature deals with the concept of intention. Turkish writer Bediuzzaman Said Nursi (1877–1960) wrote about purity of intention, suggesting that when one does service to God without sincerity and purity of intention, he implicitly commits the sin of *shirk* (associating something with God). In such a case, one is doing something for two reasons: to serve God and to serve one's own pride. He comes back to this idea of *shirk* when he writes about the various benefits that the disciplines of Sufism (*tariqa*) bring to faith. Another writer explains that purity is a singleness of intention or undivided heart.[11]

Nursi also writes about how ordinary things we do become acts of worship when we realize that this is part of our worship to God. "Intention changes ordinary acts and customs into acts of worship. It is a penetrating and pervading spirit through which inanimate states and deeds acquire life and become 'living' acts of worship."[12]

The Christian Concept of Intention

Intention is also a very important concept for Christians. The intention of the heart, more than anything else, defines our relationship with God. This concept is prominent in both the Old and New Testaments, as well as in Christian theology.

Intention in the Old Testament

The inner attitude of persons, versus outward appearance or behavior, is emphasized in a number of Old Testament passages. Though there is no specific term for this comparable to the Muslim term *niyya*, the concept is often referred to as being a "man after [God's] own heart," as exemplified in the life of King David (1 Sam. 13:14, NIV).

A Man after God's Own Heart. When God rejected Saul as king of Israel, he appointed Samuel to anoint Saul's successor (see 1 Sam. 16). Samuel went to the house of Jesse in Bethlehem and asked to see all of his sons. Samuel examined them one by one. When Samuel saw the firstborn, Eliab, he was greatly impressed and thought, "Surely the LORD's anointed stands here before the LORD" (v. 6, NIV). But God answered him with a statement that perfectly captures the Christian view of intention: "Do not consider his appearance or his height, for I have rejected him. The LORD does not look at the things people look at. People look at the outward appearance, but the LORD looks at the heart" (v. 7, NIV). Jesse presented each of his sons, and God selected none of them. However, Jesse's youngest son, David, was not present. He was tending sheep, and because he was so young, Jesse didn't bother to send for him. Finally, Samuel realized there was one more son and called for him to appear. David, the least likely candidate, was chosen by God as the next king of Israel.

David became the measuring stick for all subsequent kings that ruled Israel and Judah. When David's son Solomon turned away from God at the end of his life, we read, "For it came to pass, when Solomon was old, that his wives turned away his heart after other gods: and his heart was not perfect with the LORD his God, as was the heart of David his father" (1 Kings 11:4, KJV).

David was so highly exalted because God saw his true character and knew that even though David would fail to be perfectly obedient to God's commands, the young man had a tender heart toward and desired to please God. He was a man of childlike faith as evidenced by his willingness to confront Goliath (1 Sam. 17); he had a deep longing for the presence of God as seen in his many psalms; and when David did sin, as everyone does, he was filled with genuine remorse (see Ps. 51). The apostle Paul later characterized David's inner attitude with a phrase that may be the Christian equivalent of the term *intention:* "a man after [God's] own heart" (Acts 13:22, NIV).

A New Heart. The concept of a new heart is a recurring theme in prophetic writing. This concept also closely matches the idea of intention. Old Testament prophets were sent to minister to a wayward nation, calling the people to return to faithfulness to God. Through the prophets, God promised to bring his people back from captivity and restore them to a right relationship with him. Prophets frequently used the image of a changed or renewed heart when bringing this message of restoration. Jeremiah stated this most clearly: "I will give them a heart to know me, that I am the LORD. They will be my people, and I will be their God, for they will return to me with all their heart" (Jer. 24:7, NIV). Ezekiel also used this image frequently. He said, "I will give them an undivided heart and put a new spirit in them; I will remove from them their heart of stone and give them a heart of flesh. Then they will follow my decrees and be careful to keep my laws. They will be my people, and I will be their God" (Ezek. 11:19–20, NIV).

Mercy, Not Sacrifice. The prophet Hosea echoes the concept of intention with his statement, "For I desire mercy, not sacrifice, and acknowledgment of God rather than burnt offerings" (Hos. 6:6,

NIV). Through the prophet, God indicated that a person's inner inclination toward God is what he desires most, more than even sacrifices for sin in fulfillment of the law. Jesus himself repeated this phrase when challenging the Pharisees, who were scrupulous about obeying the letter of the law but were known to be prideful and callous toward the suffering of others (see Matt. 12:1–14).

Intention in the Gospels

Jesus had much to say about the inner life or desire of a person, the heart. He used several images to convey the idea that intention is the essence of a person's character, more important even than outward behavior.

Mouth and Heart. Jesus used the terms *mouth* and *heart* to demonstrate that there can be a disconnect between a person's inner and outer lives. Quoting the prophet Isaiah, Jesus said of his generation, "These people honor me with their lips, but their hearts are far from me" (Matt. 15:8, NIV; see Isa. 29:13). He then followed up with this teaching: "What goes into someone's mouth does not defile them, but what comes out of their mouth, that is what defiles them (Matt. 15:11, NIV). Jesus here teaches that true impurity results from evil intentions, which become evil actions, not from physical contact with "unclean" things. So purity is a matter of the heart, not the hands alone.

Whitewashed Tombs. In a scathing criticism of the scribes and Pharisees, Jesus compares them to graves that have been painted white on the outside to make them look beautiful, but inside they are filled with decaying corpses (see Matt. 23). There again he teaches the bifurcation of the outer and the inner person. Appearing clean, pure, or good on the outside does not make a person righteous. It is the condition of the heart—the intention—that indicates purity.

A Tree and Its Fruit. Jesus used the metaphor of a fruit tree to show the relationship between the heart and true character, revealed over time. He said, "By their fruit you will recognize them. Do people pick grapes from thornbushes, or figs from thistles? Likewise, every good tree bears good fruit, but a bad tree bears bad fruit. A good tree cannot bear bad fruit, and a bad tree cannot bear good fruit" (Matt. 7:16–18, NIV); he also said, "For the mouth speaks what the heart is full of. A good man brings good things out of the good stored up in him, and an evil man brings evil things out of the evil stored up in him" (12:34–35, NIV).

Behavior comes from the heart and not the other way around. A pure heart (good intention) inevitably results in good character, and an impure heart (evil intention) sooner or later results in bad behavior. Doing right doesn't make you righteous, but righteous people (those with pure intention) do right.

Jesus and the Law. The idea that intention is the essence of sin is clearly seen in Jesus's teaching on the law in the Sermon on the Mount. First, Jesus affirmed the value of the law, saying, "Do not think that I have come to abolish the Law or the Prophets; I have not come to abolish them but to fulfill them" (Matt. 5:17, NIV). Obviously, doing God's will is important. However, Jesus redefined obedience to the law by saying, "You have heard that it was said to the people long ago, 'You shall not murder, and anyone who murders will be subject to judgment.' But I tell you that anyone who is angry with a brother or sister will be subject to judgment" (vv. 21–22, NIV). Here Jesus defined sin as an act first committed in the heart—and, potentially, only in the heart. Jesus later redefined adultery in the same way, saying that lust, the inner intention of the person to commit adultery, is equivalent to the deed itself (see vv. 27–28).

The Greatest Commandment. In response to a question by his critics, Jesus gave the foundational teaching on the Christian concept of intention. The question was, "'Teacher, which is the greatest commandment in the Law?' Jesus replied: "'Love the Lord your God with all your heart and with all your soul and with all your mind." This is the first and greatest commandment. And the second is like it: "Love your neighbor as yourself." All the Law and the Prophets hang on these two commandments'" (Matt. 22:36–40, NIV). Jesus's answer, focusing in on the intention of the heart, defines the essence of doing God's will as loving God and others.

Intention in the Epistles

The apostle Paul also addresses the issue of the inner life. In his second letter to the Corinthian church, Paul writes, "Therefore we do not lose heart, but though our outer man is decaying, yet our inner man is being renewed day by day" (4:16, NASB).[13] The outer person is all that is visible—the body, behavior, circumstances. The inner person refers to the heart—attitudes, dispositions, feelings, desires, and plans. These are not visible to all. They are known only by the person and by God. And of course, intention is an aspect of the inner person. Perhaps the most frequent designation of this inner person is the use of the word *heart* (*kardia*). Author Richard Howard explains it this way:

> Often *heart* is a synonym for *within* and by implication is in contrast to that which is without. "And hope does not disappoint; because the love of God has been poured out within our hearts through the Holy Spirit who was given to us" (Rom. 5:5). Yet *heart* indicates more—it is the *center* of man, and as such is identified with understanding (cf. 2 Cor. 3:15; Eph. 1:18; 4:18) as well as man's deepest emotions (cf. 2 Cor. 8:16; Rom. 9:2; 10:1).[14]

Howard concludes, "The heart can depict both what a man *is* and the motivation for what he *does*—his character and his conduct."[15]

Several passages in the Epistles highlight the importance of inner attitudes. In Galatians, Paul talks about the fruit of the

Spirit: "But the fruit of the Spirit is love, joy, peace, patience, kindness, goodness, faithfulness, gentleness, self-control; against such things there is no law" (5:22–23, NASB). These are attitudes of the inner person, not actions of the outer person, which are governed by law. In the Ephesian letter, Paul talks about being made new in the "attitude of your minds" (4:23, NIV). Philippians 2 is another focus on the inner man. Paul writes, "Have this attitude in yourselves which was also in Christ Jesus" (v. 5, NASB). Peter expresses the same thought when he challenges readers to "arm yourselves also with the same attitude [as Christ]" (1 Pet. 4:1, NIV).

The writer of Hebrews reminds us that our attitudes or intentions are not hidden from God: "For the word of God is alive and active. Sharper than any double-edged sword, it penetrates even to dividing soul and spirit, joints and marrow; it judges the thoughts and attitudes of the heart. Nothing in all creation is hidden from God's sight. Everything is uncovered and laid bare before the eyes of him to whom we must give account" (4:12–13, NIV).

Intention in Christian Theology

Various Christian theologians have wrestled with the concept of the inner person, or intention, and its relationship to both sin and holiness.

The Concept of Sin. Simply stated, for sin to occur, it must be accompanied by intention, and intention is sin. John Wesley put this most succinctly, defining sin as a "voluntary transgression of a known law."[16] While other actions may be wrong because they harm ourselves or others or violate a command of God, guilt is not attached to them unless the doer had a conscious intention to do something known to be wrong. Other actions might be rightly called mistakes, failures, or shortcomings, but not sins. Intention is a key element of sin.

Theologian Thomas Cook asks, "If the *want* to sin is sin, may we not say that the purpose or the *want* to please God is accepted, even when we blunder and make mistakes?"[17] He then invites us to imagine a young blind girl who wants to express her love to her father, so she writes him a love note. She takes a sheet of paper and painstakingly tapes down lines of thread to help her keep a straight line. Then she takes pen and ink and begins to write. In Cook's day, writing was done with a bottle of ink and a quill made from a feather. The girl's writing was uneven, sometimes missing the line. When she failed to move the quill fast enough, it left a big blob of ink on the paper. In short, the letter was a mess, but she couldn't see that. She folded the letter and awaited her father's return from work.

When he came home, she rushed across the room to give him her "love letter" that she has so painstakingly written. Cook asks the question, "When the father receives the letter is he angry because here and there it is disfigured by a little blot or a crooked line?" Of course not! The father will cherish that letter—not because it is a literary masterpiece or displays perfect penmanship but because he knows that his blind daughter, motived by pure love, worked with all her might to tell him how much she loved him.[18]

So it is with God and us. Our efforts to please him inevitably produce mistakes and may result in a real mess. However, God looks not at the product (the outer person) but at the heart. He accepts our pure desire to please him.

Intention and Holiness. Just as Martin Luther revolutionized the church with his teaching on salvation by grace through faith, so John Wesley revolutionized the church with his teaching on holiness. One of Wesley's themes was "singleness of the eye," based on Matthew 6:22–23 (KJV): "The light of the body is the eye: if therefore thine eye be single, thy whole body shall be full of light. But if thine eye be evil, thy whole body shall be full of darkness. If therefore the light that is in thee be darkness, how great is that darkness!" Wesley wrote, "'The eye is the lamp of the body:' And what the eye is to the body, the intention is to the soul."[19] In his treatise *A Plain Account of Christian Perfection,* Wesley again made the connection between intention and holiness. He wrote, "Have a pure intention of heart, a steadfast regard to his glory in all your actions."[20] He identified three benchmarks of the meaning of Christian perfection, and they are all inner qualities: (1) a "purity of intention," (2) having the mind of Christ, and (3) "loving God with all our heart."[21] Theologian Mildred Bangs Wynkoop states that purity is "a single-hearted, unalloyed love for God."[22] Melvin Dieter put it succinctly: "Christian perfection is purity of intention."[23]

A novice archer is a helpful metaphor for understanding the relationship between intention and both sin and holiness. Imagine an archer aiming at a distant target. Some of the arrows will hit the target, and a few might even hit the bull's-eye. But many will miss the target altogether. Other people can see the target and judge the archer by the accuracy of each shot. If all the shots miss the target, we would say he is a terrible archer. God, however, looks at the heart. If the archer aims for the bull's-eye but misses, it is a bad shot but not a willful misdeed. God knows the difference; other people do not. God judges the intention of the archer (inner person), not the result of the shot (outer person).

Building on the Plank of Intention

There is a great deal of similarity between the Muslim and Christian understandings of intention. In fact, this may be the point at which the two faiths are the most alike. First, both assign a great deal of importance to an individual's intention or purpose, which is a feature of the inner person. Second, both define sin in terms of intention. If there is no intentionality behind an act, then it is classed as a mistake, error, or forgetfulness. Though the act may bring consequences, it does not bring guilt before God. Third, both hold that God is the one who can and will judge internal intentions. God knows all things. This is not the case with other people. They know only what is visible; God judges the heart. Fourth, there is a connection between intention and purity. The King James Version speaks of the "single" eye, which the *New International Version* translates as the "healthy" eye (see Matt. 6:22). Perhaps that is a better translation, but it does not capture the imagination as "single" eye does. Al-Ghazzali and other Muslim writers also use this phraseology in writing about how "singleness of heart or intent" shows purity.[24]

Intention is the first plank on our bridge of understanding, and it is a strong one. Both Christians and Muslims understand that human beings are full of frailties and weaknesses. We cannot live free of errors and mistakes. It is not possible that every arrow we shoot will hit the bull's-eye. Yet Christians desire to love God, and Muslims have the intention to submit to God. That is a good place for dialogue to begin.

8
PLANK TWO: HOLINESS
—

The concept of intention is a solid plank for our bridge of understanding. A second plank is the concept of holiness. Both Christians and Muslims speak a great deal on this subject. Though we understand it in slightly different ways, it is a shared goal. We both want to become holy. Let's begin by learning about the Muslim view of holiness.

Muslim View of Holiness

The concept of holiness in Islam rests on two ideas. The first is that of *al-Insan al-Kamil*—the "perfect man." The other is the idea of holiness itself. Since Sufism is the branch of Islam most concerned with the inner aspects of the faith, most writers on these subjects are Sufis, though the concepts are known throughout Islam. We begin with the idea of the perfect man.

The Perfect Man

The perfect man, according to twelfth-century writer Muhammad ibn al-'Arabi, was the visible manifestation of God on earth. "The Perfect Man is that human individual who has perfectly realized the full spiritual potential of the human state."[1] He was a perfect man inhabited by the perfect God. Another writer, 'Abd al-Karim al-Jili, states that "one must not lose sight of the fact that the essence of this Unique Being is identical to the Divine Essence, so that there cannot be divergence between him and God. One may say that he does not do what God would not have done, or that God acts through him."[2] Other writers state: "The Perfect Man is precisely the human self at its final stage of perfection and completion. For man there is nothing conceivable beyond this state."[3] And he is a "whole man" who is marked by "perfection of being."[4] He is "the norm of all spiritual perfection."[5]

Metaphors for the Perfect Man. The perfect man is fleshed out by Muslim writers using a variety of interesting metaphors.

- **Copy of God:** The perfect man is one in whom God's names and attributes are perfectly expressed.[6]
- **Mirror:** Muhammad, as the perfect man, reflects God.[7]
- **Water and Ice:** The divine essence is like water, which crystallizes on earth into ice but always has the tendency to turn back into water. When God is completely realized in the heart and life of a person, that person becomes the embodiment of the divine as well as the perfect human. As water is drawn upward into the heavens, so the perfect man is drawn to become one with God.[8]
- **Isthmus:** The perfect man is an isthmus between God and the world, embracing attributes of both.[9]
- **Cross:** This may be the most interesting metaphor to Christians. The perfect man is "complete and perfect." *Complete* refers to horizontal progress of the person, and *perfect* refers to vertical. They meet together in the perfect man.[10]

Muhammad Is the Perfect Man. Muslims agree that Muhammad was the perfect man: every good and perfect thing was embodied in him. The Turkish Sufi writer Said Nursi, in his *Epitomes of Light,* accords many exalted names to Muhammad indicating his unique position among all men.

Saints Are the Perfect Man. Many Sufis hold to the idea that others in addition to Muhammad were the perfect man. Some say that every prophet beginning with Adam up through Muhammad has been a perfect man. Some hold that *shaykhs* (Sufi master teachers) are examples of a perfect man and that there must be a perfect man in every age. Shi'a consider a leading imam a perfect man.

Anyone Can Become a Perfect Man. Some Muslims teach that, theoretically, anyone can become a perfect man. While this possibility has only been actualized by the prophets and saints, it is a possibility for all.[11]

The Idea of Holiness

The concept of holiness exists in Islam, though the term itself is not as common as in Christianity. Mahmoud Ayoub states:

> This is not to say that the Qur'an has no concept of holiness; rather, it calls it by different names. A holy life is one that is guided by God to the straight way, a balanced course between the extremes of each facet of human life. . . . A holy person is one who enjoins the good and dissuades from evil. A person who purifies him- or herself by prayers, almsgiving, and other works of righteousness is a holy person.[12]

There are several aspects of the Muslim understanding of holiness. By understanding these different aspects, we get a fuller picture of what holiness means to Muslims. Watch for the obvious parallels to the Christian concept of holiness, which we will explore in a moment.

Longing for God. Muslim writer Faruqi notes that there is a restlessness in humanity. "This state of restlessness of human soul is due to its origin in the Infinite Soul."[13] Humanity belongs to God and longs to return to him. One of the themes of Sufi mysticism is the circular journey of the soul. Humanity comes down to the earth as the representative of God in heaven. But as pictured in the water and ice metaphor, the soul of humanity is "drawn" back to God and begins the journey back to its source.

Death of the Carnal Self. Despite the fact that Muslims do not accept the idea of original sin, both the Qur'an and the *ahadith* suggest that human beings have a bent toward evil. The Qur'an says humans are created weak or frail (Qur'an 4:28, Yusuf Ali), and one commentator says that idea can be translated, "The soul is indeed obliged evilwards" or "The self is under a conducing towards wrong."[14] A *hadith* says that, except for Jesus, "no child is born but that Satan touches it when it is born whereupon it starts crying loudly because of being touched by Satan."[15] What does this touch of Satan mean? It seems to indicate something similar to what David said when he cried out, "Behold, I was shapen in iniquity; and in sin did my mother conceive me" (Ps. 51:5, KJV).

Sufis write much about the soul (*nafs*). The faithful are admonished to "fear the place of his Lord and hinder the *nafs* from lust" (Qur'an 79:40).[16] The Turkish Sufi Nursi talks about "purifying the carnal soul."[17] Sufis teach that there are three levels or stages of the soul. To a Christian ear, this sounds suspiciously like a doctrine of original sin. The lowest level is the Uncontrollable Soul. "The soul is prone to evil" (Qur'an 12:53, Ahmed Ali). The next level of the soul is the Self-Accusing Soul. This is the conscience. "And I swear by the spirit that blames itself" (Qur'an 75:2, Ahamed). The final level of that soul is the Soul at Rest. "O you soul who are at rest! Return to Your Lord, joyful and pleasing in His sight" (Qur'an 89:27–28).[18] Another term that comes up frequently in Sufi literature is that of *fana*, which can best be translated "dying to self."

Purity. One of the daily requirements for a devout Muslim is to pray five times each day. At the back of each mosque are faucets. The faithful who come for prayer perform the *wudhu*, which is the ceremonial cleaning of the body prior to entering the presence of God in prayer. It is an elaborate ritual involving cleaning the face, feet, and hands. It is intended to be more than just external cleansing. As he is washing his body, the Muslim prays, "[O] God, purify my inner self along with my outer body. In this way, the earnest prayer [pray-er, or one who prays] makes his soul clean too, like his body."[19] Khan compares these two cleansings and says, "The purity of one's heart is, however, far more important than that of the body."[20]

Love. The great Muslim writer al-Ghazzali felt that love is central to understanding holiness. "Human perfection resides in this, that the love of God should conquer a man's heart and possess it wholly, and even if it does not possess it wholly, it should predominate in the heart over the love of all other things."[21]

Another perceptive Muslim writer, Abou el Fadl, explains how love for God molds one's views: "To love God, a person must love all that God loves and dislike all that God dislikes. . . . In short, it is impossible to love God or be beloved by God and not to exhibit the characteristics of Godliness."[22]

A Pure Heart. In one *hadith* Muhammad speaks of the importance of the heart: "There is a piece of flesh inside man's body. When it is purified, the whole body gets purified; when it is impure, the whole body remains impure. That piece is the heart."[23] When the heart is pure, then it becomes the dwelling place for God. The Sufi Nasr uses Old Testament terminology when he talks of the *shekinah* glory of God tabernacling within the human heart.[24]

A Christian Conception of Holiness

Holiness is at the core of the Christian faith. Both the Old and New Testaments speak relentlessly on the subject, making the concept of godliness or Christlikeness (expressed in a variety of ways) inseparable from biblical Christianity. In Genesis Abraham is told to "walk before Me, and be blameless" (17:1, NASB). In Leviticus the Israelites are to "consecrate [themselves] and be holy, because I am the LORD your God" (20:7, NIV). The psalmist cries out, "Wash away all my iniquity and cleanse me from my sin. . . . Cleanse me with hyssop, and I will be clean; wash me, and I will be whiter than snow" (Ps. 51:2, 7, NIV). Isaiah speaks of the "Way of Holiness" (35:8, NIV), and Ezekiel tells the Jews in exile that God will give them a "new heart" and "new spirit" and will cleanse them from their impurities (Ezek. 36:25–27, NIV).

New Testament passages are copious, comprehensive, and compelling on the subject of holiness. Jesus said, "Therefore you are to be perfect, as your heavenly Father is perfect" (Matt. 5:48, NASB). And the most important of all the commandments is, "Hear, O Israel: The Lord our God, the Lord is one. Love the Lord your God with all your heart and with all your soul and with all your mind and with all your strength" (Mark 12:29–30, NIV). Jesus prayed for his disciples, "Sanctify them by the truth; your word is truth" (John 17:17, NIV).

The epistle writers, too, dwell on the subject of holiness. The apostle Paul writes, "Since we have these promises, dear friends, let us purify ourselves from everything that contaminates body and spirit, perfecting holiness out of reverence for God" (2 Cor. 7:1, NIV), and the writer of Hebrews urges, "Follow peace with all men, and holiness, without which no man shall see the Lord" (Heb. 12:14, KJV). "Come near to God and he will come near to you. Wash your hands, you sinners, and purify your hearts, you double-minded," says James (James 4:8, NIV), and Peter states, "But just as he who called you is holy, so be holy in all you do; for it is written: 'Be holy, because I am holy'" (1 Pet. 1:15–16, NIV). The apostle John promises, "If we confess our sins, he is faithful and just and will forgive us our sins and purify us from all unrighteousness" (1 John 1:9, NIV).

Clearly, the idea of holiness is vital to the Christian faith. But what does the term *holiness* mean? Here are several aspects of holiness, beginning with the meaning of the word itself. Again, notice the significant overlap with the Muslim concepts of the perfect man and holiness.

Wholeness. The word *holy* comes from the same old English word form that means "whole." "Holiness is the state or condition of being holy, whole, healed."[25] Holiness is a defining characteristic of God. H. Orton Wiley writes, "We may say then, that holiness belongs to the essential nature of God in a deeper and more profound sense than merely as one attribute among others."[26] God is holy, complete, lacking nothing.

Purity. Holiness and *purity* are closely connected terms. *Purity* refers to something that is unadulterated, having no other substance or contaminant within it. As one writer puts it, "It is God's total aversion to sin and unrighteousness that makes holiness practically synonymous with moral purity in later Old Testament writings and throughout the New Testament."[27] Purity also characterizes the love that Jesus spoke of in his explanation of the greatest commandment: "Love the Lord your God with all your heart and with all your soul and with all your mind" (Matt. 22:37, NIV). In the Sermon on the Mount, Jesus said, "Blessed are the pure in heart, for they will see God" (5:8, NIV).

Perfect. The word *perfection* is a biblical term. We are told to go on to "perfection" (Heb. 6:1, KJV). Jesus said, "Be perfect, therefore, as your heavenly Father is perfect" (Matt. 5:48, NIV), and Paul urges, "Let us therefore, as many as be perfect, be thus minded: and if in any thing ye be otherwise minded, God shall reveal even this unto you" (Phil. 3:15, KJV). God is perfect, and we are to be perfect as he is. Perfection is the goal of holiness. This is not a flawless perfection but perfection in the sense that we are fully fit for the purpose God desires of us. What God desires, as the next term indicates, is that we love him with all our being and our neighbor as ourselves. By doing this we are perfect in the biblical sense.[28]

Love. The apostle John wrote, "God is love" (1 John 4:16, KJV), and because God is love, we, too, live in love. John continues, "He that dwelleth in love dwelleth in God, and God in him. Herein is our love made perfect, that we may have boldness in the day of judgment" (vv. 16-17, KJV). Christians are commanded to "love the Lord your God with all your heart and with all your soul and with all your mind" (Matt. 22:37, NIV).

Sanctification. To be sanctified is to be made holy, which is God's will for every person. Paul writes, "For this is the will of God, even your sanctification, that ye should abstain from fornication: That every one of you should know how to possess his vessel in sanctification and honour" (1 Thess. 4:3–4, KJV); he also affirms, "God hath from the beginning chosen you to salvation through sanctification" (2 Thess. 2:13, KJV). Perhaps the strongest statement on sanctification in the New Testament is found in 1 Thessalonians 5:23: "And the very God of peace sanctify you wholly" (KJV). This word *wholly* intensifies the meaning of holiness as whole, complete, or entire.[29]

Sinless. Though some Christians debate this aspect of holiness, we all agree that followers of Christ are to be like him, that is, to be *Christlike.* Jesus was the perfect man, completely holy, living a sinless life. John states, "My dear children, I write this to you so that you will not sin" (1 John 2:1, NIV), and Paul asks, "What shall we say, then? Shall we go on sinning so that grace may increase? By no means! We are those who have died to sin; how can we live in it any longer? . . . because anyone who has died has been set free from sin" (Rom. 6:1–2, 7, NIV). One aspect of holiness, then, is moral purity or freedom from sin. This is the goal of every believer.

Building on the Plank of Holiness

The concept of holiness is a second area of broad overlap in Christian and Muslim thought. This will form a broad plank for our bridge of understanding, though more so between Christians and Sufi Muslims. To summarize, here are five solid points of contact between Islam and Christianity related to the concept of holiness.

First, both Muslims (particularly Sufis) and Christians acknowledge the concept of a *perfect person*. These ideas are primarily applied to Muhammad and Jesus, respectively. However, branches of both faiths hold the possibility that ordinary people can become, in some sense, the perfect person. On the Muslim side, this idea is most clearly expressed by the twelfth-century writer 'Arabi and expounded two centuries later by al-Jili. In Protestant Christianity, the concept of *Christian perfection* is best articulated by eighteenth-century evangelist John Wesley. This is a point on which some Muslims disagree with one another, and some Christians do to. Even so, it makes a good beginning for a dialogue on the concept of holiness.

Second, both Muslims (again, especially Sufis) and Christians speak of a longing of the heart to know God and to be close to him. Muslims believe that humankind was created in God's image and came to earth but longs to return to God, the heart's true home. The great Augustine expressed for all Christians this desire to be one with God: "For Thou has formed us for Thyself, and our hearts are restless till they find rest in Thee."[30] The concept of longing for union with God is a point of contact for both faiths.

Third, both Muslims and Christians desire to overcome the carnal nature. Though Muslims believe that human beings are born sinless, they see sin as inevitable. Christians, too, desire to escape the corruption of the sinful nature. Though we do not use the red-flag terms *inbred sin* or *sinful nature* in dialogue with Muslim friends, we can speak of the inclination of the soul to do evil and our common desire to rise above that to live without sinning.

Fourth, both faiths include the concept of dying to self. Muslims describe this as *fana*. The Muslim writer Faruqi referred to love as the "great killer," meaning that love for God means the death of self, a concept nearly identical to the teachings of Jesus and Paul.[31]

Fifth, both Muslims and Christians emphasize the idea of purity as an aspect of holiness. Muslims speak of both inner and outer purity, evidenced by their washing before prayer with the intention of purifying both body and spirit. Christians also teach the need for outer purity (moral behavior) and inner purity (a heart devoted to God).

When building a discussion on the plank of holiness, remember that these concepts are more prominent with some Muslims than others. Also, our purpose in dialogue is not to persuade but to enlighten both ourselves and our Muslim friends. A discussion of holiness and its related concepts is an ideal place to further our understanding of one another. In the next chapter, we'll discuss the third—and most surprising—plank in our bridge of understanding.

9
PLANK THREE: STRUGGLE
—

Our third plank of commonality between Islam and Christianity will be surprising to many. It is the concept of *struggle*, or *striving*, which Muslims call *jihad*. This is one of the most controversial subjects in the world today, particularly between Islam and the Western world. The very word *jihad* is as inflammatory to Christians as the word *crusade* is to Muslims.[1] Both terms are emotionally charged. For most Westerners, jihad is an entirely negative concept. It causes Westerners to think of the September 11 attacks or other acts of violence committed in the name of religion. However, to most Muslims jihad is seen as a positive thing. *Jihad* would best be translated as "struggle" or "effort," and it denotes a striving on all fronts: spiritual, political, social, personal, military, and economic.[2] No matter how it is defined, jihad is understood by most Muslims as a positive struggle for the cause of Allah. For this reason, when the Western press attaches the word *terrorism* to jihad, it is deeply offensive to Muslims.

In Islam, there are two aspects to the concept of struggle: *greater jihad* and *lesser jihad*. The difference is illustrated by a *hadith* in which a group of Muslim fighters are returning home after a successful battle. Muhammad greets them, welcoming them back from the "lesser jihad" and challenging them to get involved in the "greater jihad," the struggle against their passions.[3] Thus the idea of two types of jihad has been firmly established in Muslim thinking from the very beginning: an outer jihad is undertaken with the hand or sword, and an inner jihad is the spiritual battle in the heart of each Muslim.[4]

Lesser Jihad

Outer jihad, or "*jihad* with the sword," is what most Christians think of when the subject of jihad is raised. Admittedly, there is little overlap between this concept of jihad and Christianity. However, it is important to understand outer jihad because it is a prominent part of Islam and a topic of great concern today. There are four supports in Islam for the doctrine of jihad with the sword: the life of Muhammad, the Qur'an, the *ahadith*, and the Muslim concept of the world.

Muhammad and Jihad

The initial community of Muslims was carved from a hostile society and immediately had to fight, literally, for its existence. The Muslims faced enemies on all sides: the Meccans, Bedouin tribesmen, Jewish clans, Byzantines, and Persians. The exact number of battles that Muhammad himself fought is estimated between twenty-seven and seventy-eight. At the Battle of the Ditch in 627, some nine hundred were killed. The children and wives of the enemy were taken as wives by the Muslims or sold into slavery. Muhammad himself took one of the women who had just been widowed and made her his wife. This has been a difficult part of history for Muslims to defend.

After the death of Muhammad, the Muslims spread throughout the Middle East by military conquest. Within a few decades, their borders stretched from India to Spain. Many reasons are offered for this rapid expansion—political, military, and religious. Muslims have always pointed to these early decades of spectacular growth and victory as divine proof that Islam is right. Thus there has always been strong support based on the life of Muhammad and the early Muslims for the idea of jihad as a military struggle.

The Qur'an

The Qur'an gives an "uncertain sound" about jihad. One can find support for just about any position on the subject, which is confusing to Westerners. Moderate Muslims, who advocate peace and freedom, claim support for their position based on the sura that says, "There is no compulsion in religion" (2:256, al-Hilali). Suicide bombers also claim that what they are doing is supported by the Qur'an, pointing to the "Sword Verse," Sura 9:5: "When the sacred months are over slay the idolaters wherever you find them. Arrest them, besiege them, and lie in ambush everywhere for them. If they repent and take to prayer and render the alms levy, allow them to go their way. God is forgiving and merciful" (Dawood). Each side claims that its passages abrogate the verses of the other side. The traditional viewpoint is that in the beginning, when Muhammad and the few Muslims were a tiny minority in Mecca, the revelations Muhammad received called for compromise and nonconfrontation. However, as the Muslim community began to grow in strength, the revelations become more and more strident and militant.

The Ahadith

There are several stories that support Muslim warriors fighting for God's cause. Bukhari relates a *hadith* in which Muhammad says, "I would love to be martyred in Allah's Cause and then get resurrected and then get martyred, and then get resurrected again and then get martyred and then get resurrected again and then get martyred" (4:54).[5] Another *hadith* promises that when a person is martyred for the cause of Allah, "his sins are pardoned," "he is" given a "seat in paradise," "he is safe from the punishment of the grave and the terror of judgment," "a crown of dignity is placed on his head," "he is married to seventy dark-eyed virgins," and he can make "intercession for seventy of his relatives."[6]

Muslim View of the World

Another factor contributing to the concept of militant jihad is the way Muslims see the world. Traditionally, Muslims have seen the world as divided into two parts. First is Muslim territory (*dar al-Islam*). Second is the territory of war (*dar al-harb*). In the traditional understanding, everywhere that is not Muslim territory is a place of disorder, lawlessness, strife, and ignorance. Some moderates recognize a third category, the territory of treaty (*dar al-sulh*). As the name implies, this is a neutral area where a peace agreement has been reached.

The Silent Majority

The number of Muslims who support or engage in jihad with the sword is a small minority of Muslims. One question often voiced by Westerners is this: "If the majority of Muslims do not support the activities of these jihadists, why don't they speak out?" Here are some common reasons for silence among the majority of Muslims who do not condone violent jihad.

First, many moderate Muslims agree with the ends of the jihadists but not their means. The radicals would like to create a world where God's laws are honored and obeyed. Moderates agree with this as an ideal, so they may find it difficult to speak against the jihadists. Second, some fear retribution. A Muslim living in the freedom of a Western country who has family members living in a Muslim country might be reluctant to take a stand that might bring repercussions upon his family. Third, Muslim moderates are sometimes silent because they do not wish to be seen as Western lackeys or disloyal to their own culture and faith.

It should be noted that the "silent majority" is not always silent. Often, those who do speak out in opposition to violence are not heard. Bad news makes the news, while good news is ignored. So a letter written by Osama bin Laden promising death to America gets much media coverage. Yet few have heard of the A Common Word initiative, an effort by moderate Muslims to bring peace and understanding between Christians, Muslims, and Jews.

Greater Jihad

Armed conflict is the concept that most Westerners think of when hearing the word *jihad*. However, the "greater jihad" is the struggle for purification of the heart. As one writer puts it, "The greater, and one might also say greatest . . . *jihad* is therefore the inner battle to purify the soul of its imperfections, to empty the vessel of the soul of the pungent water of forgetfulness, negligence, and the tendency to evil."[7] Another states, "The greatest *jihad* is the struggle of every person against the evil of their own carnal soul."[8] This meaning of the term *jihad* is virtually unknown to Westerners but forms our third plank of commonality with Islam.

Jihad as Striving

The idea of struggle and striving is inseparable from the greater jihad. There are several Qur'anic verses that speak to the importance of striving, including, "Man can have nothing but what he strives for" (Qur'an 53:39, Yusuf Ali), and "We have created man into toil and struggle" (Qur'an 90:4, Yusuf Ali).

The book *Forty Stations*, written in the eleventh century by a Sufi master named Abu Sa'id ibn Abul-Khayr, identifies a pathway of stations marking the spiritual progress of a Sufi Muslim. Christians would identify these stations as spiritual disciplines. This pathway is a long journey of effort, striving, and discipline. It begins with the discipline of intentions and moves on through thirty-nine others, including conversion, repentance, discipleship, struggle, patience, contentment, surrender, worship, truthfulness, hope, annihilation of self, sanctity, love, service, and truth.[9]

Jihad as a Lifelong Endeavor

The inner struggle for purity of intention is a lifelong endeavor for the Muslim. As one writer states, it is a jihad within oneself in which one expends the maximum effort to control "arrogance, jealousy, greed, revenge, anger, etc.," and this jihad is a "permanent feature of the life of a believer, continuing day and night, and ending only with death."[10]

Christian View of Struggle

The concept of *jihad*, or "struggle," may seem an unlikely point of contact between Christians and Muslims, especially given the violent overtones of this term to Westerners. However, the concepts of discipleship, disciple, self-mortification, and lifelong striving for Christlikeness are familiar to Christians and not dissimilar from the concept of inner jihad. We will focus on the parallels between Christian discipleship and inner jihad; however, it may be noted that Christians, too, hold to the ideal of advancing the kingdom of God throughout the world, which has at times included a struggle for peace and justice, such as during the abolition and civil rights movements in the United States. Though we reject the idea of advancing God's kingdom through violence, we do have a Great Commission to "make disciples of all nations" (Matt. 28:19, NIV). In that sense, we are involved in the "effort" to win the world for Christ.

The Necessity of Human Effort

Salvation is a gracious gift of God that is appropriated through faith in Jesus Christ. The apostle Paul unequivocally states, "For by grace are ye saved through faith; and that not of yourselves: it is the gift of God: Not of works, lest any man should boast" (Eph. 2:8–9, KJV). Though we are not saved by our own righteousness or good works, the Scriptures are filled with admonitions for Christians to produce "fruit," that is, to display a changed lifestyle after coming to Christ. We are equipped to do good works, and God expects that of us.

It is possible to live without sin, but there is discipline and effort involved in avoiding it. When people came out to the desert to be baptized by John the Baptist, his message was straightforward: "Produce fruit in keeping with repentance" (Matt. 3:8, NIV). It is one thing to confess with the mouth that one is a Christian, but it is another thing to produce "Christian" fruit. Jesus said, "So every good tree bears good fruit, but the bad tree bears bad fruit. A good tree cannot produce bad fruit, nor can a bad tree produce good fruit" (Matt. 7:17–18, NASB). If this metaphor is applied to a Christian life, this means that one who professes to be a Christian must produce "Christian" fruit, and if he or she does not produce "Christian" fruit, then he or she is not a Christian.

Paul wrote, "For it is not those who hear the law who are righteous in God's sight, but it is those who obey the law who will be declared righteous" (Rom. 2:13, NIV). And the writer of Hebrews says, "And let us consider how we may spur one another on toward love and good deeds" (Heb. 10:24, NIV). Jesus himself was definite on this subject, saying, "Not everyone who says to me, 'Lord, Lord,' will enter the kingdom of heaven, but only the one who does the will of my Father who is in heaven" (Matt. 7:21, NIV).

Clearly, God expects good works from us, and this is not accomplished without effort on our part. In his eleventh discourse on the Sermon on the Mount, John Wesley reinforced that theme based on Luke 13:23–24: "He [Jesus] said unto them, Strive to enter in at the strait gate: for many, I say unto you, will seek to enter in, and shall not be able" (KJV). Wesley challenged his listeners to "strive, in all the fervor of desire, with 'groanings which cannot be uttered.'" He concludes,

> "Strive to enter in at the strait gate," and only by this agony of soul, of conviction, of sorrow, of shame, of desire, of fear, of unceasing prayer; but likewise by ordering thy conversation aright, by walking with all thy strength in all the ways of God, the way of innocence, of piety, and of mercy. Abstain from all appearance of evil: Do all possible good to all men: Deny thyself, thy own will, in all things, and take up thy cross daily. Be ready to cut off thy right hand, to pluck out thy right eye, and cast it from thee; to suffer the loss of goods, friends, health, all things on earth, so thou mayest enter into the kingdom of heaven![11]

Striving for the Sake of the Gospel

Twice in his letter to the Philippians, Paul talks about striving for the sake of the gospel. "Whatever happens, conduct yourselves in a manner worthy of the gospel of Christ. Then, whether I come and see you or only hear about you in my absence, I will know that you stand firm in the one Spirit, striving together as one for the faith of the gospel" (Phil. 1:27, NIV). And later, "Yes, and I ask you, my true companion, help these women since they have contended at my side in the cause of the gospel" (4:3, NIV). Also, Paul wrote in Romans, "I urge you, brothers and sisters, by our Lord Jesus Christ and by the love of the Spirit, to join me in my struggle by praying to God for me" (15:30, NIV).

Jesus stressed this concept also, in his parables of the lost sheep and lost coin. The shepherd and the woman looked for the sheep and coin until they were found (Luke 15:1–10). In the Sermon on the Mount, Jesus encourages his disciples to be proactive. "Ask and it will be given to you: seek and you will find: knock and the door will be opened to you. For everyone who asks receives; the one who seeks finds; and to the one who knocks, the door will be opened" (Matt. 7:7–8, NIV). We are expected to pursue God and pursue others in completion of his work. Jesus said, "Whoever wants to be my disciple must deny themselves and take up their cross and follow me" (16:24, NIV).

Peter speaks of the struggle for holiness, saying,

Through these he has given us his very great and precious promises, so that through them you may participate in the divine nature, having escaped the corruption in the world caused by evil desires. For this very reason, make every effort to add to your faith goodness; and to goodness, knowledge; and to knowledge, self-control; and to self-control, perseverance; and to perseverance, godliness; and to godliness, mutual affection; and to mutual affection, love. For if you possess these qualities in increasing measure, they will keep you from being ineffective and unproductive in your knowledge of our Lord Jesus Christ. (2 Pet. 1:4–8, NIV)

We have a responsibility to be active in seeking God, doing his will, and living transformed lives.

The Lifelong Journey

We are saved by grace through faith, a definite work of God's grace. And there is a second work of grace that occurs when a Christian whose sins have been forgiven surrenders his or her heart completely to the control of the Holy Spirit. This act of consecration results in a heart filled with love for God (Matt. 22:37), and that person is no longer "double-minded" (James 1:8, NIV). This is a pure heart.

However, purity is not the same as maturity. Christian purity happens instantaneously when a heart is totally surrendered to God. Christian maturity develops through the lifelong process of drawing closer to Christ. As we do, we become more and more like him. This is not an easy thing; it means carrying your cross daily. This involves discipline, continued self-sacrifice, and ongoing effort in cooperating with the Holy Spirit. Maturity takes time.

Spiritual Disciplines

Another important area of a Christian's inner struggle is spiritual disciplines. Perhaps no contemporary writer has written more persuasively on the subject than Richard Foster in his landmark book titled *Celebration of Discipline*. Foster states, "Superficiality is the curse of our age. The doctrine of instant satisfaction is a primary spiritual problem. The desperate need today is not for a greater number of intelligent people, or gifted people, but for deep people."[12] Foster then evaluates the change that these disciplines will bring in one's life.

> No longer is there the tiring need to hide our inner selves from others. We do not have to work at being good and kind; we *are* good and kind. It would be work to refrain from being good and kind, because goodness and kindness are part of our nature. Just as the natural motions of our lives once produced mire and dirt, now they produce the fruit of the Spirit.[13]

Foster identifies twelve disciplines divided into three categories (though some writers identify a few more). There are Inward Disciplines: meditation, prayer, fasting, and study. There are Outward Disciplines: simplicity, solitude, submission, and service. And there are Corporate Disciplines: confession, worship, guidance, and celebration.[14] Discipline is hard work; it takes commitment, striving, and continued effort. If we are to be the persons that God has called us to be, we will carry our cross of discipline.

Building on the Plank of Struggle

The idea of jihad, defined as the struggle to do the will of God, is the third plank for our bridge of understanding between Muslims and Christians. However, there are two things to keep firmly in mind when using this plank to dialogue with a Muslim friend.

Caveats

First, it is vital to remember that we are speaking of the greater jihad, or internal striving, and not the lesser jihad, or jihad by sword—that is, war. Though both faiths hold the spreading of God's kingdom throughout the earth, Christians firmly reject violence as a means of doing so.

Second, it is extremely important to remember the difference between Christians and Muslims on the purpose or end result of the struggle. Muslims hold to the idea that they will make it to heaven based on their good works. They undertake the inner jihad as a way of earning heaven. Christians have an entirely different purpose in mind for striving. We believe that we are saved by God's grace alone, through faith. Good works have nothing to do with the free gift of salvation. However, we desire to "produce fruit in keeping with repentance" (Matt. 3:8, NIV). We want to live a new and different life that is pleasing to God, and this requires continued effort on our part. So for both Christians and Muslims, the inner struggle is very important but for fundamentally different reasons.

Nailing It Down

With those points firmly in mind, we can use the concept of the greater jihad as a strong addition to our bridge of understanding.

Striving. The Muslim life requires effort. Praying five times a day takes much time and effort. I once visited a Muslim professor right at prayer time. His house is located adjacent to the neighborhood mosque, so the call to prayer reverberated through the house. This was the first time we had met, and I encouraged him to go ahead to prayer. He explained that he was caught in a bind because the Qur'an explains that prayer is an important obligation, but being a good host to a visitor is also an important obligation. I assured him that I would watch the house for him, so he and his wife went to prayers and I waited for them. It meant that both of them had to change clothes, perform the *wudhu* (ritualistic washing to cleanse one's body), walk to the mosque, perform the prayer, walk back, change clothes again, and then resume normal activities. This is to be done five times a day. Then there are the other obligations, such as paying the *zakat* (alms) and performing the *hajj* (pilgrimage to Mecca). All of these things are expensive in time, energy, and finances.

Christians also see the need for effort in pursuit of holiness, though not in a legalistic fashion. When one invites Jesus into his or her heart, things change. Paul explained that "if anyone is in Christ, the new creation has come: The old has gone, the new is here!" (2 Cor. 5:17, NIV). This means that we do not live as we used to live. We have new habits and new disciplines. Jesus said, "Whoever wants to be my disciple must deny themselves and take up their cross and follow me" (Matt. 16:24, NIV). This concept of self-denial is very important, and it is hard work—and sometimes very costly.

Good Works. For Muslims, good works are essential because of the *mizan* (scale) that awaits each person upon death. It is important that Muslims do enough good works to outweigh the bad if they hope to make it to heaven. For Christians, the injunction to "produce fruit in keeping with repentance" (Matt. 3:8, NIV) is taken seriously. Good works do not earn salvation, but once a person has become a "new creation," good works are essential. A good tree will produce good fruit.

Purity. The greater *jihad* is the effort to purify one's inner self: one's intentions as opposed to one's actions. Christians also prize the idea of inner purity. Christian perfection is, among other things, purity of heart or a singleness of intention.

Cleansing the Carnal Nature. Though Muslims do not believe in the concept of original sin, they do understand the notion of the *carnal soul.* Greater jihad is a war against this carnal soul. Christians are very familiar with the concept of the carnal nature. We recognize that there is both a cleansing of the carnal nature (the crisis of purity) as well as a disciplining of the recalcitrant self (the process of maturity).

Struggle, or jihad, is a surprising point of commonality between Muslims and Christians. In many ways we are able to "speak each other's language," a great advantage in building a bridge of understanding. Now that we have established both the piers of general commonality between Christians and Muslims (history, Scripture, theology, and mission) and three strong planks for our bridge (intention, holiness, and struggle), we can get practical about establishing a dialogue with Muslim friends. In the next section, we'll establish guidelines and offer practical tips for taking the first steps on your bridge of understanding.

Part III

Building a Bridge
of Understanding

10
PRACTICAL ADVICE
FOR BRIDGE BUILDERS

—

The first part of this book explained who Muslims are, some of their key doctrines, and supports for these beliefs. We discovered a chasm of theological and historical differences between Muslims and Christians. Then we identified four general areas of commonality between Christians and Muslims. Though these general commonalities sometimes contain differences within them, they are strong supports, or piers, for building our bridge of understanding. We also discovered three more specific areas of faith and practice in which there are much greater similarities between us: intention, holiness, and struggle. These concepts form solid planks to lay across our bridge.

Yet bridge building is a very practical—and, in some ways, individual—enterprise. At some point, hopefully, you will put down this book and enter a conversation with a Muslim friend. How will you go about that? What can you do to build on the knowledge you now have about Islam and its similarities (and differences) to Christianity? In this chapter we identify some dos and don'ts as well as answer some questions you may have about beginning a dialogue with a Muslim friend. We will talk about these areas:

- Building Trust and Respect

- How to Meet Muslim Friends
- Spending Time Together
- Starting Spiritual Conversations

When we are finished, you'll have a greater level of confidence that you can meet, get acquainted with, and build a friendship with a Muslim friend or neighbor. This is your practical start at becoming a bridge builder.

Building Trust and Respect

In creating a bridge of understanding, showing respect and building trust are essential. If you have a nominal acquaintance with a Muslim, perhaps at school, work, or in your neighborhood, you may be eager to see that relationship develop into a friendship. To build the trust and respect necessary for friendship to develop, keep these things in mind.

Never Criticize Muhammad or the Qur'an

Westerners in general, and Western Christians in particular, find certain things about the life of Muhammad and the Qur'an puzzling or even offensive. However, criticism of either is totally off limits for those interested in building bridges instead of walls. Westerners place a high value on the rights of the individual, so we may feel that anyone has the right to express his or her opinion on any subject. Freedom of speech is one of our most cherished values. Muslims, however, are united in feeling that any criticism of their beloved Prophet or the Qur'an is highly offensive and demands a response. Therefore, bridge builders understand that any criticism of Muhammad or the Qur'an should be kept to oneself when visiting with a Muslim.

This does not mean that we ignore or whitewash the serious objections we have, but we do keep our opinions to ourselves as a sign of respect to our friends. If asked what we think about the

Qur'an, one could respond, "I know it is your sacred book, and I know that it has some valuable instructions on how we should live." If asked about Muhammad, one might answer, "I know that he is your Prophet. I believe that he did his best to live as he felt God wanted him to. He felt that God was giving him an important message that he was responsible to share with his people." The bridge builder does not need to compromise his or her own beliefs, but neither should he or she feel the need to articulate all the reasons why Christians cannot accept the Muslim understanding of Muhammad and the Qur'an.

Dialogue; Don't Debate

Some of us probably shy away from anything that smacks of an argument, so we avoid debates quite naturally. Others look forward to any opportunity to forcefully present their opinions or defend their convictions. Generally, there are no winners in a debate over religion, only losers. Bridge builders are interested in dialogue but will pass on debate. Rather than scoring points with brilliant repartee, they will score points with careful listening and thoughtful responses.

Handle Your Bible Carefully

The Scriptures should be handled carefully, especially around Muslim friends. This is literal, not metaphorical, advice. My own parents were pastors and later missionaries. The Bible was a prominent part of our home, and we all had our own Bibles. We never put our Bibles on the floor, and we never put other books or other things on top of our Bibles. To us, this was part of honoring and respecting God's Word. Muslims very much feel the same way about the Qur'an. It is never handled carelessly. They have a special wooden cradle to hold the Qur'an when they are reading it. They would never let the Qur'an touch the floor. When they finish reading it, they wrap it in a cloth and carefully store it. Thus, if you have Muslims in your home, make sure that you treat your own Bible with the same respect that they would treat the Qur'an. Muslims are likely to find it puzzling and offensive to see the Bible treated carelessly.

Observe Boundaries in Cross-Gender Communication

In Western societies interaction between men and women is more open and freer than in Muslim countries, where there are often protections in place for women. This could be something as simple as the *hijab*, a veil covering the head and shoulders, or as elaborate as the *burka*, which covers the woman from head to toe. It could mean that a woman must be accompanied by a male relative to go anywhere in public. While most of these restrictions are not observed in Western societies, some are. Muslim women in the West often wear head coverings. And it would be considered inappropriate for any man to initiate conversation with a veiled Muslim woman, even in a public place. A male who is not a close relative would never enter the home of a Muslim woman if her husband were not present, and the reverse would also be true.

If you have the opportunity to host a Muslim man, make sure that he would never be invited to arrive at your home when only women were present. The golden rule of conversation in the Muslim world is that men converse with men, and women with women. If you are living next to a Muslim family, and you have developed a friendship, then cross-gender communication would be acceptable. However, it would still be inappropriate for an unmarried man and woman to be alone together.

Put Away Dogs and Pork

Muslims do not eat pork and do not like to be around dogs. If you invite Muslim friends to your home for a meal, they won't assume that you understand or practice their *halal* (kosher) rules. However, serving pork would never be acceptable and must be avoided at all costs. If you have a dog, put it away when you are entertaining Muslim friends. Dogs are considered unclean by many Muslims. Being around one would be offensive; being licked by one would be abhorrent.

How to Meet Muslim Friends

Now that you have a desire to be a bridge builder—and some basic idea of how to relate to a Muslim friend—you need to meet some Muslims if you don't know any already. What is the best way to establish a relationship with a Muslim friend? Your living circumstances and community may determine the answer to that question. Generally speaking, Muslim women are more identifiable (assuming they wear some form of head covering). Muslim men normally won't have distinctive dress and would be best identified by their name. Beyond that, here are some practical possibilities for establishing contact with Muslims near you.

Meet through Your Kids. If you have children in school, find out if any of their classmates have Muslim names or come from countries that are predominantly Muslim. Do any Muslim parents attend PTA meetings or other school events? Your children may already have friends from Muslim households. Interacting with the parents of your children's friends is one good place to start.

Check Nearby Universities. Students come from all over the world to study in North America, including many from Muslim countries. If you live near a university, find out if they have a hospitality program for international students and request students from predominantly Muslim countries. In many ways international students are like displaced persons. They are separated from family, friends, and support networks. They are eager for friendship and sometimes need hospitality. Students may be more open to building relationships while here than they would be in their home countries.

Patronize Muslim Businesses. Support and visit any local businesses that might be owned or run by Muslims. Sole proprietorships such as convenience stores, gas stations, and restaurants would be a good place to start.

Visit a Mosque or Muslim Community Center. If your community has a mosque or Islamic center, visit and become acquainted with people who are attending activities there.

Aid Refugees. Are there any refugee areas around you? Helping refugees is one of the greatest things you could do. They are some of the most needy and most appreciative people you will ever meet. There are tremendous opportunities for bridge building with them.

Spending Time Together

What can you do with a Muslim friend? What activities might you do? The short answer is simple: anything you can imagine that observes the guidelines already noted. Indeed, one's imagination is just about the only limit on the possibilities. Here are a few possibilities to get you started. For a much more exhaustive list, you could check out Fouad Masri's excellent book titled *Hummus, Haircuts, and Henna Parties.*[1]

Meet a Need

If your Muslim friend has just arrived in America or in your community, he or she will have a plethora of needs. Helping someone become established in a new community is an excellent way to build a friendship. Here are a few things you might assist with:

- *Shopping.* Show your friend the best place to shop for groceries, hardware, clothing.
- *Getting a Driver's License.* Everyone could use help navigating the bureau of motor vehicles. Offer to go along and guide the process.

- *Finding Professionals and Service Technicians.* Share what you know about the best doctors, auto mechanics, or plumbers.
- *Translating.* If you are bilingual, you could be an invaluable resource to an immigrant or international student by translating documents, helping to fill out applications, or reading instructions.
- *Dealing with Government.* Immigration issues, taxes, permits—all can be complicated even for citizens. You might be able to help a Muslim friend deal with a government agency or at least offer moral support.
- *Family Needs.* Babysitting, providing transportation, assistance with moving, bringing in a meal—be alert for any way you can help people in need.

Men's Activities

Remember that Muslims are very gender sensitive. Some bridge-building activities are more male oriented, so if you are male, look for opportunities to spend time with a Muslim man. Consider inviting your friend to participate in a sports league. (Remember that in most countries outside of North America, soccer is the favorite sport.) Invite him to join the gym or health club where you are a member. Offer to take him hunting, fishing, or camping.

Women's Activities

The bridge-building opportunities among women may be even greater. The point of these activities is to provide a reason for you to spend time together in a way that will further a friendship. Some of these activities would also apply to male-male friendships.

- English tutoring
- Working out at a women-only health club or event
- Invitation to a cosmetics or home-décor party
- Teaching one another cooking
- Learning a craft together, such as sewing or scrapbooking

- Driving lessons
- Shopping
- Going out for lunch
- Walking or biking

Family Activities

Muslims are very family oriented. A number of years ago, a survey was conducted to determine Indonesians' highest values. Not surprisingly, family topped the list. Family activities are great bridge-building opportunities for your Muslim neighbors. Here are some ways to spend time together as a family.

- Play dates for your children at the park
- Going to a museum
- Taking in a ballgame
- Celebrating cultural events, such as Independence Day or Canada Day
- Children's sports leagues
- Babysitting swap
- Tutoring children

Remember that if Muslim neighbors entrust their children to you, do not look on this as an opportunity to evangelize them. Also, avoid television programs or video games that are not entirely family friendly.

The Golden Rule of Hospitality

Hospitality is one of the greatest values for people in the eastern part of the world. The Bible is set in the Middle East, and the value of hospitality is seen prominently in many Bible stories. When the three angels were on their way to check out Sodom and Gomorrah, they passed by Abram's tent, and he compelled them to stop for lunch. When the angels reached Sodom, Lot was there and compelled them to come to his house (see Gen. 18–19). Whenever Elisha visited Shunem, a family there "constrained" (2 Kings

4:8, KJV) him to have a meal with them. They even had a special room added to their house just to accommodate him whenever he passed by. To this day, Middle Easterners in general, and Muslims in particular, place a high value on hospitality. That makes hospitality one of the best ways to build a bridge to your Muslim neighbors. Invite your Muslim friends to your house for a meal, and accept an invitation to dine at their house as well.

Because this is such a valuable bridge, I offer some advice. If you eat at a Muslim home, the meal will be a veritable feast. The wife will have spent hours preparing it. It will be a very relaxed time of eating and visiting. When you go, make sure that you bring a gift of some kind. It could be something for the house, or flowers, candy, or fruit.

When you invite Muslims to your home for the meal, the menu is important. As a rule, Western Christians don't have religious taboos connected to food preparation or consumption. We might have dietary restrictions, but not religious ones. That is not the case for Muslims. If you know your Muslim friends well enough, it is a good idea to clear your menu with them first—wife to wife. It would be memorably painful for them to either refuse to eat or, more likely, go ahead and eat but never forget it.

Also, make sure that you plan and prepare properly. Don't rush home after work, throw something in the microwave, and expect that you will have laid a strong foundation for a bridge of understanding. Make a special occasion of the meal. This does not mean you should never invite them over for a backyard cookout—there is a time for that too. But if you are inviting them for a nice dinner at your home, take the time to do it right. They will appreciate the effort, and you will be rewarded with open doors of friendship. They will see the meal as a sign that you like them enough to sacrifice time and effort for them.

Spiritual Conversations

Our goal is to breach the walls of fear and hatred that too often characterize our relationship with Muslims and to build a bridge of understanding. We want to create a new chain of responses that leads from understanding to acceptance, from acceptance to appreciation, from appreciation to respect, from respect to love. Eventually, that will include more than simply getting acquainted with your Muslim neighbors and sharing a meal. You will want to turn your conversations to spiritual matters. Hopefully, your friends will too. Here are some practical tips for engaging your Muslim friends in a conversation about faith.

Pray

We have not talked yet about the vital importance of prayer in this entire effort of bridge building. When we pray, we trust God to guide us. We pray that he will open doors and we will see the open door and have the courage to walk through it. Pray for your Muslim friends, not for their salvation only but also for the practical needs in their lives. Pray also for opportunities to speak about matters of faith. Trust God to provide the right time and the right words to say.

Commit Time to This Effort

Time is another key ingredient of bridge building. While there are other factors, a key differentiation between an acquaintance and a friend is the amount of time spent together. It takes time to build a meaningful friendship. From that seedbed of friendship, the flowers of trust and spiritual sharing will grow.

Be Open and Vulnerable

You cannot hope for openness and vulnerability on your friend's part if you don't exhibit them yourself. A great way to move in that direction is to be authentic about your own spiritual life and progress. You might begin with a sentence like this: "I don't know about you, but I have found . . ." Your openness and vulnerability will call for the same from them.

Remember the Importance of Dreams and Visions

Dreams and visions are an important source of spiritual authority in the Muslim world. If your Muslim friends have a memorable dream, they will not be afraid to attach spiritual significance to it. This is one of the key ways that God has been reaching into the Muslim world. There are many testimonies of Muslims who have become followers of Jesus because they had a dream or vision of him. So if your Muslim friend wants to tell you about a dream he or she just had, don't brush it off. Take the time to listen carefully, and if you see spiritual significance in this dream, try to help your friend understand that God may be reaching out to him or her through it.

Ask Practical Questions

Fouad Masri suggests several practical questions to open a conversation, which can easily move into a faith conversation.

- What country are you from?
- How long have you been in this country?
- Can you tell me about where you are from?
- What is the best thing about your country?
- What did you like and dislike about growing up there?
- What do you like about this country?
- What did you like about being raised a Muslim?
- What was your most difficult experience as a child?
- Did you know any Christians growing up? What was your opinion of them?
- How do you practice your religion? Which practices mean the most to you personally?
- What holidays (or Eids) do you participate in?

- Why do you think there are different religions?
- Who is Jesus, in your opinion? How did you learn this about Jesus?
- What have you heard about Jesus? How do you know those facts are true?
- Have you read the Injeel (New Testament), which is the revelation given to Jesus?[2]

You Can Do This!

If you are like most people, you have a feeling of excitement about the prospect of becoming a bridge builder but also a sense of trepidation. Forming a friendship with people of another culture and religion may seem intimidating. Perhaps you fear making a mistake or looking foolish. Or you may wonder what to say or do after "Hello."

Relax. You can do this. Pray for God's guidance, and follow the Spirit's leading. Being a bridge builder will take some time and effort, and, yes, you will make mistakes along the way. Don't let that frighten you. The relationship between Christians and Muslims is one of the most urgent matters facing our world—and you are in a position to do something about it. I believe you have what it takes to build a first-class bridge of understanding. I'm praying that you will step out and do exactly that.

In our closing chapter, I will show you why bridge building is such an urgent matter and give you a few final guidelines for overcoming our own cultural blindness and for engaging friends in a meaningful interfaith dialogue.

11

A COMMON WORD
BETWEEN US AND YOU

—

We began this book by examining the chasm that too often separates Christians and Muslims. Let us end it with an appeal for openness and dialogue on both sides. The third sura of the Qur'an is titled *Al 'Imran* (The Family of Imran). In verse 64, Muhammad reaches out to the Jewish and Christian communities by appealing to the commonalities between the three groups.

Say: "O People of the Book! come to common terms as between us and you: That we worship none but Allah; that we associate no partners with him; that we erect not, from among ourselves, Lords and patrons other than Allah." If then they turn back, say ye: "Bear witness that we (at least) are Muslims (bowing to Allah's Will)." (Yusuf Ali)

Based on this verse, a group of prominent Muslims in 2008 set up an initiative called A Common Word between Us and You. They noted that the sacred scriptures of both faiths speak to the importance of seeking peace and harmony. From the Qur'an: "Allah commands justice, the doing of good, and liberality to kith and kin, and He forbids all shameful deeds, and injustice and rebellion" (Qur'an 16:90, Yusuf Ali). And from the Bible: "Blessed are the peacemakers . . ." (Matt. 5:9, KJV). They also cite this often-quoted Qur'anic passage: "If God had pleased He could surely have made you one people (professing one faith). But He wished to try and test you by that which He gave you. So try to excel in good deeds. To Him will you all return in the end, when He will tell you of what you were at variance" (Qur'an 5:48, Ahmed Ali).[1] I add my voice to those of this group, and many others, to urge understanding, cooperation, and peace between Christians and Muslims. In the remaining pages of this book, I hope to inspire you to join this effort of bridge building—and believe it can be accomplished.

The Butum Tree

Ghazi bin Muhammad, a prince of the royal family of Jordan and a founding member of the "A Common Word" initiative, speaks of a large *butum* tree that stands in the Jordanian desert. There are no other trees for miles around, and the tree is said to be fifteen hundred years old. The prince recalls that at the start of the "A Common Word" initiative, he and several scholars met under the shade of this tree and prayed to God that their peace initiative would achieve its goals. He speculated that this may have been the very tree that figured in one of the early traditions concerning Muhammad's childhood and that this tree could also have borne witness to one of the earliest meaningful contacts between Christians and Muslims. Now, it was the starting place for this latest attempt to find common ground between the world's two greatest religions.[2]

How inspiring to think that this ancient tree of God's own planting might symbolize the similarities between the great peoples who acknowledge him as the one true God. As the "A Common Word" manifesto points out, both Christians and Muslims are instructed to love God, and both faiths stress the importance of loving one's neighbor. Love of God and love of one's neighbor—certainly there is "a common word" between us.

The Urgency of Understanding

Christians and Muslims together comprise 55 percent of the world's population. If we cannot find peace between us, there can be no peace on the earth.

Finding common ground between Muslims and Christians is not simply a matter for polite ecumenical dialogue between selected religious leaders. . . . our common future is at stake. The very survival of the world itself is perhaps at stake. . . .

So let our differences not cause hatred and strife between us. Let us vie with each other only in righteousness and good works. Let us respect each other, be fair, just, and kind to another and live in sincere peace, harmony, and mutual goodwill.[3]

These sentiments expressed by "A Common Word" founders are true. There is common ground between us, and we urgently need to build on this common ground. We must find ways to meaningfully engage each other in conversation that is not superficial, polemic, or mutually accusatory, but rather a conversation that touches the deepest recesses of our hearts and souls. We must listen to one another and allow that listening to blossom into understanding, respect, and love.

A Place to Start

To further equip you as a bridge builder, I turn to the wisdom of two eminent scholars, one a Muslim and the other a Christian. Each believes in the need for openness, relationship building, and understanding between Christians and Muslims, and each suggests guidelines for creating such dialogue. As we have done so often in this book, we will see great similarities between the heart and mind of these two men of different faiths. Both offer good advice to would-be bridge builders.

A Muslim Viewpoint: Goals for Dialogue

Muslim scholar Mahmoud Ayoub[4] suggests several goals that Christians and Muslims should maintain in dealing with each other. First, there must be a "mutual acceptance of the legitimacy and authenticity of the religious tradition of the other as a divinely inspired faith."[5]

Second, we "must accept each other as friends and partners in the quest for social and political justice, theological harmony, and spiritual progress"[6] toward God. Third, we must see each other "as an equal partner—and not an opponent—in dialogue."[7] Fourth, we must let each tradition speak for itself. This means that we must really listen to each other and understand what they are saying rather than proceed according to what we *think* they mean. Finally, we must be fair and objective when comparing the two faiths.[8]

Ayoub goes on to say that there are three types of dialogue in which we should engage. There is the *dialogue of life,* which simply means living together as friends and neighbors. Then there is the *dialogue of beliefs,* in which we learn what the other believes. Third, there is the *dialogue of da'wa,* which Christians would call witnessing. There is nothing wrong with this. If you are confident that you have found the right path, you need to share that good news. Finally, there is what Ayoub calls the *dialogue of faith.* This is interaction at a deeper level: dialogue regarding struggles, difficulties, and anxieties as well as sources of deep satisfaction found in one's faith. The emphasis here is on deep, open, and honest sharing.[9] It is difficult to accept the faith of another person. We each look at each other's faith through the lens of our own and tend to only see the deficiencies of the other's tradition and the superiorities of our own.[10] Yet this dialogue is immensely important.

A Christian Viewpoint: Guidelines for Face-to-Face Encounter

Christian scholar M. Darrol Bryant[11] also believes that we need an interfaith encounter and dialogue between Christians and Muslims. If this is to take place, he suggests that four things must happen. As a prospective bridge builder, take special notice of the similarities to Ayoub's viewpoint.

- Each community must be allowed to interpret itself.
- Each must listen to the other and attempt to understand them on their own terms.
- We must recognize that we are both fellow human beings and pilgrims in the journey of faith.
- There must be a sharing at the deepest level, not just superficial things.[12]

Bryant concludes that "the appalling ignorance of the West concerning Islam" can be remedied only through face-to-face meetings of Christians and Muslims and education.[13]

Rules to Build By

Both Ayoub's and Bryant's guidelines will serve you well as a bridge builder. It may be helpful to summarize the similarities between them. As you construct your bridge of understanding, remember these rules to build by.

First, each community must be allowed to interpret itself. Muslims must be allowed to explain and interpret Islam, and Christians must be allowed to do the same for Christianity.

Second, there must be genuine acceptance of each other as a partner in dialogue, not an opponent in debate.

Third, we must recognize that we are both fellow pilgrims in an unfriendly world, trying to bring God's message of peace, equality, and freedom to people who often don't want to hear what we are saying.

Fourth, be willing to share at the deepest level of life and faith. There must be openness and vulnerability.

To Build a Bridge

We began this book by examining the chasm that often separates Muslims and Christians. That there are differences, and that those differences have been a source of misunderstanding, animosity, and even violence, cannot be denied. My hope is that you and I, and the legion of bridge builders who will join us, can be agents of change as we reach out to our Muslim neighbors. Muslims used to be the people who lived in far-off lands and were never seen. Now they live all around us. Many are immigrants, but many more call North America their native home. Yet, sadly, most Americans know very little about Islam,[14] and the view Americans have toward Muslims has become increasingly negative since 9/11.[15] Many Americans say they would not want a Muslim neighbor.[16] However, other research shows that Americans who know at least one Muslim are more likely to hold positive views of Muslims and Islam than those who don't.[17] If there is to be a bridge of understanding, we must be the ones to lay the first plank.

This does not mean that we accept all claims of Islam or ignore the differences between us. As Bryant puts it, "In the dialogue between religions we are called not to reduce the intensity of depth of our own faith but to bear witness to it while respecting the faith of the other."[18] We do not believe that Islam is a superior religion. We do not believe Muslims have God's final revelation for humankind. But neither do we see them as hopelessly lost heretics. There are things that we can learn from them, such as their unabashed willingness to take a stand for God and their spiritual disciplines of prayer and fasting. There are many bridges of similarity between us that can enable us to engage in meaningful interaction.

Paul wrote about the walls separating Jews and Gentiles, and his words apply to the walls between Christians and Muslims as well: "But now in Christ Jesus ye who sometimes were far off are made nigh by the blood of Christ. For he is our peace, who hath made both one, and hath broken down the middle wall of partition between us" (Eph. 2:13–14, KJV). Let us be those who break down the walls of hostility and build a bridge of understanding.

And so we close this book at the very place we began, with a quotation by a Muslim, pleading for mutual understanding: "The Tree of Fear grows in the Land of Ignorance."[19] We are all too familiar with the chain of negative responses born of ignorance: ignorance creates prejudice, prejudice leads to suspicion, suspicion produces fear, fear ignites hatred, and hatred breeds violence. My prayer is that God may enable you to build a bridge of understanding that will reverse that chain of negative responses and instead bring openness, acceptance, appreciation, love, and peace.

GLOSSARY

—

abrogation. The doctrine that a Qur'anic verse revealed at a later time than another verse can abrogate, or cancel, the earlier revealed verse.

'Ashura. Anniversary of the Battle of Karbala, the day in which Shi'a Muslims remember the defeat of Husayn by the forces of the Umayyad caliph Yazid in AD 680.

caliph (Arabic, *khalif*). A person considered a political and religious successor to the prophet Muhammad and a leader of the entire Muslim community.

caliphate. A form of Islamic government led by a caliph (or *khalif*).

dar al-harb. The abode of war, comprised of regions that are in conflict, that do not enjoy the peace of Islamic governance.

dar al-Islam. The abode of Islam, comprised of those regions under governance of Islam.

hadith (plural: *ahadith*). A story about what Muhammad said or didn't say or do that has become an example for Muslims to follow.

hajj. A pilgrimage to a sacred place; the Great Hajj is an annual pilgrimage to Mecca, which is required once in the lives of all able-bodied and financially capable Muslims as a pillar of Islam.

hijra. Muhammad's flight from Mecca to Medina, marking year zero in the Muslim calendar.

i'jaz. The doctrine of the inimitability of the Qur'an, meaning that no book can be compared to the Qur'an in its beauty and teachings.

ijma'. The consensus of fellow Muslim scholars.

ijtihad. The use of reason to arrive at a spiritual truth.

al-Insan al-Kamil. The perfect man or the universal man.

Islam. The religion established by Muhammad, one of the world's great religions.

islam. Submission to Allah.

jahiliyya. The time of ignorance prior to the coming of Muhammad and God's law.

jihad. Striving or struggle.

kafir. An unbeliever.

khutba. A sermon delivered in mosques at noon on Fridays.

mihrab. The prayer niche around which the mosque is organized for prayers that indicates the direction of Mecca.

Muslim. An adherent of the religion of Islam.

muslim. One who has submitted to Allah.

nafs. Soul.

niyya. The intention to do something.

qadim. The doctrine of the eternality of the Qur'an.

qibla. The direction of Mecca toward which one faces for *salat* five times each day.

qiyas. A technique used by Muslim judges in which they seek analogies from the Qur'an to use in their rulings.

Qur'an (or Koran). The sacred scriptures for Muslims.

Rashidun Caliphate. The first four "rightly guided" rulers to follow Muhammad, who were both political and religious leaders, viewed similarly to the "righteous" kings of Judah.

Salafiyya. A modern movement seeking a return to the state of affairs in seventh-century Arabia, the time of the Rashidun Caliphate.

salat. Prayer, one of the Five Pillars of Islam, of which there are five prayer times each day; the Door of Prayer is also an entryway to heaven.

sawm. A fast, the most important of which is the sunup to sundown fast of the month of Ramadan, which is one of the Five Pillars of Islam.

shari'a. Literally the path to water; refers to God's laws.

Shi'ite. A member of the group that supported 'Ali, the nephew of Muhammad, and wanted him to succeed Muhammad as ruler of the Muslims.

shirk. The greatest sin, which is assigning a partner to God.

shura. A consultative council, such as a committee called to determine who should succeed a deceased ruler.

Sufi. Literally a wearer of wool (*suf*), it refers to Muslims who stress the inner aspects of the Muslim faith.

sunna. The example of life set by Muhammad.

Sunni. The majority branch of Islam.

sura. A division of the Qur'an, comparable to a chapter in the Bible.

tariqa. The path of discipline followed by Sufi disciples.

tawhid. The doctrine of the *unicity* of God, meaning that God is one and has no partner.

umma. A collective understanding of the Muslim people (similar to the "people of God").

zakat. Charity toward others, one of the Five Pillars of Islam.

NOTES
—

Introduction

1. Muhammad Arif Zakaullah, *The Cross and the Crescent: The Rise of American Evangelicalism and the Future of Muslims* (Kuala Lumpur, MY: Other Press, 2004), flyleaf.

Chapter 1: Who Are the Muslims?

1. Karen Armstrong, *Islam: A Short History* (New York: Modern Library, 2002), 11.

2. *Encyclopedia of Islam*, 2nd ed., s.v. "Ka'ba," accessed April 26, 2017, http://referenceworks.brillonline.com/entries/encyclopaedia-of-islam-2/kaba-COM_0401?s.num=0&s.f.s2_parent=s.f.book.encyclopaedia-of-islam-2&s.q=ka%27ba.

3. As hardliners, these reformers prefer that today's lifestyles be exactly like those of seventh-century Arabia.

4. *Islam* (spelled with a capital *I*) refers to the religion of Islam, whereas *islam* (lowercase *i*) refers to the idea of submission to God.

5. Muhammad was related to the Khazraj tribe through his father's mother. His great-grandfather, Hashim, married a woman from this tribe.

6. The term *successor* or *khalif* is the technical term for the leaders who followed Muhammad.

7. In many books on Islam, two dates are used. For example, the date of death for the great theologian al-Ghazzali is AH 505, 1111 CE. So we understand that he followed Muhammad by about five hundred years, which helps trace the development of Muslim thought and juxtapose it with Western thinkers and movements.

8. J. J. Saunders, *A History of Medieval Islam* (New York: Routledge, 1972), 30.

9. P. De Lacy Johnstone, *Muhammad and His Power* (New York: Charles Scribner's Sons, 1908), 143.

Chapter 2: The Rise of a World Religion

1. Martin Lings, *Muhammad: His Life Based on the Earliest Sources* (1983; repr., Cambridge: Islamic Texts Society, 2007), 345.

2. Mark A. Noll, *Turning Points: Decisive Moments in the History of Christianity* (Grand Rapids: Baker Books, 1997), 120.

3. Hasanuddin Ahmed, *A Concise History of Islam* (New Delhi: Goodword Books, 2008), 205–18, 264–77, 398–406.

4. M. Ali Lakhani, *The Sacred Foundations of Justice in Islam: The Teachings of 'Ali ibn Abi Talib* (Bloomington, IN: World Wisdom, 2006), 23.

5. Mahmoud M. Ayoub, *Islam: Faith and History* (London: Oneworld, 2004), 142.

6. David Waines, *An Introduction to Islam* (Cambridge: Cambridge University Press, 1995), 228.

7. How many messages have been preached in our churches challenging the members to "go back to the New Testament church" and live as they did?

Chapter 3: How Muslims Think

1. Toshihiko Izutsu, *God and Man in the Qur'an* (Kuala Lumpur, MY: Islamic Book Trust, 2002), 195.

2. Farid Esack explains this in his book *The Qur'an: A Short Introduction* (Oxford, UK: Oneworld, 2002), 31–32.

3. *Encyclopedia of Islam*, 2nd ed., s.v. "hadith."

4. Abdulaziz Sachedina, *The Islamic Roots of Democratic Pluralism* (New York: Oxford University Press, 2001), 18.

5. Bukhari's collection actually contains approximately 7,397 separate *ahadith*, many of which are parallel transmissions of the same account, or around 2,602 individual stories (*Wikipedia*, s.v. "Ṣaḥīḥ al-Bukhārī," last modified October 4, 2016, https://en.wikipedia.org/wiki/Sahih_al-Bukhari, citing Jonathan A. C. Brown, *Hadith: Muhammad's Legacy in the Medieval and Modern World*, Foundations of Islam [Oxford, UK: Oneworld, 2009], 32).

Chapter 4: The Five Pillars of Islam

1. The Eight Doors to Paradise include the Door of Prayer, the Door of Charity, the Door of the Hajj, and the Door of Rayyan (for those who fast).

2. A historical understanding of the Five Pillars of Islam can be found in Albert Hourani's *A History of the Arab Peoples* (Cambridge, MA: Harvard University Press, 1991), 147–51. This chapter takes into account the perspective of Hourani.

3. When men and women worship in the same location, women worship behind the men so that they are not a visible distraction to the men.

4. Hotel rooms in Indonesia will each have an arrow affixed to the ceiling pointing in the proper direction for prayers.

5. While in Christian tradition people often place importance on participation in one's local church, in Islamic tradition the importance is placed on being part

of a *jami'* mosque anywhere. For most Sunni Muslims, to be a part of the *umma*, or "community" in general, is more important than to be a part of a particular fellowship.

6. Obtaining permission from the mosque's imam before such a visit is advisable.

7. *Wikipedia*, s.v. "Zakat," last modified September 7, 2016, https://en.wikipedia .org/wiki/Zakat.

8. *Encyclopedia of Islam*, 2nd ed., s.v. "*Djizya*."

9. The article *Wikipedia*, s.v. "Islamic taxes," last modified August 26, 2016, https://en.wikipedia.org/wiki/Islamic_taxes, gives a somewhat unnuanced look at these taxes. The article "Jizya," OMICS International, http://research.omicsgroup .org/index.php/Jizya#Rate_of_jizya_tax, explains Islamic taxes in more detail.

10. The Alexandrian calendar is followed by Coptic Christians in Egypt and Coptic Christians in Ethiopia (*Wikipedia*, s.v. "Coptic calendar," last modified September 12, 2016, https://en.wikipedia.org/wiki/Coptic_calendar). The five to six "complementary days" in the French Revolutionary calendar functioned similarly (*Wikipedia*, s.v. "Sansculottides," last modified December 4, 2015, https:// en.wikipedia.org/wiki/Sansculottides).

Chapter 5: What Separates Us

1. Timothy George, *Is the Father of Jesus the God of Muhammad?* (Grand Rapids: Zondervan, 2002).

2. I recognize that it is not possible to rate the attributes of God. He is perfect in all of his attributes, and they are all equally important. I formulate the proposition in this way in the effort to identify the different perceptions of the two faiths.

3. Bill Musk, *Kissing Cousins?* (Oxford, UK: Monarch Books, 2005), 147.

4. Paul Enns, *The Moody Handbook of Theology* (Chicago: Moody Publishers, 2014), 452.

5. Chawkat Moucarry, *Faith to Faith* (Nottingham, UK: InterVarsity Press, 2001), 179–80.

6. *Rasul Allah wa Kalimatuhu* (Sura 4:171), literally, "a messenger of God and his word."

7. Moucarry, *Faith to Faith*, 141.

8. Ibn Warraq, "Introduction" in Ibn Warraq, ed., *What the Koran Really Says* (Amherst, NY: Prometheus Books 2002), 41–58.

9. Chawkat Moucarry, *The Prophet and the Messiah* (Downers Grove, IL: InterVarsity Press, 2001), 245.

10. Emir Fethi Caner and Ergun Mehmet Caner, *More than a Prophet* (Grand Rapids: Kregel Publications, 2003), 55.

11. Because of Christ's sacrifice, grace is made available to all people from birth, granting the free will to respond in faith to God. Thus, "every human being . . . is in a state of grace," though "not everyone is in a state of saving grace" (Samuel M. Powell, *Discovering Christian Faith* [Kansas City: Beacon Hill Press of Kansas City, 2008], 166). See also note 12 below.

12. God's "reaching out" to all people and his enablement of their freedom to choose is called prevenient grace by some Christian traditions. The term *prevenient grace* means "grace that goes before."

Chapter 6: Piers of Commonality

1. Norman L. Geisler and Abdul Saleeb, *Answering Islam* (Grand Rapids: Baker Books, 1993), 213.

Chapter 7: Plank One: Intention

1. "Labbaika Allahumma Labbaik—Talbiyyah of the Prophet," *Sisterinhijab* (blog), October 7, 2012, http://www.sisterinhijab.munirah.co.uk/creatives/labbai ka-allahumma-labbaik-talbiyyah-of-the-prophet/.

2. Ibn Rajab al-Hanbali, *The Compendium of Knowledge and Wisdom* (London: Turath Publishing, 2007), xiii.

3. Ibid., 2.

4. Ibid., 10. This *hadith* is credited to Abu 'Imran al-Juni.

5. Ibid., 25.

6. Ibid.

7. Ibid., 10.

8. Ibid., 645.

9. Ibid., 647.

10. Imam al-Ghazzali, *Ringkasan Ihya' Ulumuddin*, ed. Abu Fajar al-Qalami (Surabaya, IDN: Gitamedia Press, 2003), 396. The translation from Indonesian to English was done by the author.

11. Abu Hamed Muhammad al-Ghazzali, *On Truthfulness and Sincerity*, trans. Jay R. Crook (Chicago: Great Books of the Islamic World, 2002), 34.

12. Bediuzzaman Said Nursi, *Al-Mathnawi al-Nuri: Seedbed of the Light* (Somerset, NJ: Light, 2007), 113.

13. See also Rom. 2:28–29 and 7:22.

14. Richard Howard, *Newness of Life* (Kansas City: Beacon Hill Press of Kansas City, 1975), 23.

15. Ibid.

16. John Wesley, *The Works of John Wesley*, 3rd ed. (1872; repr., Peabody, MA: Hendrickson Publishers, 1984), 11:396.

17. Thomas Cook, *New Testament Holiness* (1903; repr., Salem, OH: Schmul Publishers, 1978), 10.

18. Ibid.

19. Wesley, *Works*, 7:297.

20. Wesley, *Works*, 11:368.

21. Ibid., 444.

22. Mildred Bangs Wynkoop, *A Theology of Love* (Kansas City: Beacon Hill Press of Kansas City, 1972), 338.

23. Melvin E. Dieter et al., *Five Views on Sanctification* (Grand Rapids: Zondervan Publishing, 1987), 27.

24. Al-Ghazzali says that if our intention is one or single, then it is pure, but if there are two intentions, then it is mixed and not pure (*Al-Ghazzali on Truthfulness and Sincerity*, trans. Muhammad Nur Abdus Salam, ed. Seyyed Hossein Nasr [Chicago: Great Books of the Islamic World, 2002], 53).

Chapter 8: Plank Two: Holiness

1. R. W. J. Austin, introduction to *The Bezels of Wisdom*, by Ibn al-'Arabi (ca. 1200; repr., Mahwah, NJ: Paulist Press, 1980), 37.

2. 'Abd al-Karim al-Jili, *The Universal Man*, ed. and trans. Titus Burckhardt (Roxburgh, UK: Beshara Publications, 1995), 58n108.

3. William C. Chittick, "The Perfect Man as Prototype of the Self in the Sufism of Jami," *Studia Islamica* 49 (1979): 137.

4. Frithjof Schuon, *Understanding Islam* (Bloomington, IN: World Wisdom Books, 1998), 122–23.

5. P. K. Koya, ed., *Hadith and Sunnah: Ideals and Realities* (Kuala Lumpur, MY: Islamic Book Trust, 1996), 276.

6. Kenneth Cragg, *Muhammad and the Christian* (Maryknoll, NY: Orbis Books, 1984), 60.

7. Seyyed Hossein Nasr, *Science and Civilization in Islam* (Cambridge, MA: Harvard University Press, 1968), 348.

8. R. A. Nicholson, *Studies in Islamic Mysticism* (1921; repr., Cambridge, UK: Cambridge University Press, 1967), 84–85.

9. Ibid., 152–53.

10. Ayatullah Shaheed Murtadha Mutahhari, *The Perfect Man* (Mumbai, IND: Baab-e-Ilm Islamic Institute, 2005), 8.

11. Seyyed Hossein Nasr, ed., *Islamic Spirituality: Foundations* (New York: Crossroad Publishing, 1987), xxii.

12. Mahmoud Ayoub, "A Muslim Appreciation of Christian Holiness," *Islamochristina* 11 (1985): 97.

13. "Colloquium on Holiness in Islam and Christianity, Rome, 6-7, May 1985," *Islamochristina* 11 (1985): 16.

14. Kenneth Cragg, *The Mind of the Qur'an* (London: George Allen and Unwin, 1973), 97.

15. Phil Parshall, *Inside the Community* (Grand Rapids: Baker Books, 1994), 152.

16. Quoted in Annemarie Schimmel, *Mystical Dimensions of Islam* (Chapel Hill, NC: University of North Carolina Press, 1975), 112, Internet Archive, https://archive.org/stream/137665622MysticalDimensionsOfIslamAnnemarieSchimmel/137665622-Mystical-Dimensions-of-Islam-Annemarie-Schimmel#page/n133/mode/2up.

17. Nursi, *Al-Mathnawi al-Nuri,* 373.

18. Ahmad A. Galwash, *A Handbook of Muslim Belief* (New Delhi: Goodword Books, 2001), 241–42.

19. Maulana Wahiduddin Khan, *Principles of Islam* (New Delhi: Goodword Books, 2003), 120.

20. Ibid., 167.

21. Abu Hamed Muhammad al-Ghazzali, *The Alchemy of Happiness*, trans. Claud Field (London: Octagon, 1980), 25, cited by Roland E. Miller, *Muslims and the Gospel: Bridging the Gap* (Minneapolis: Lutheran University Press, 2005), 82.

22. Khaled Abou el Fadl, *The Great Theft* (San Francisco: HarperSanFrancisco, 2007), 133–34.

23. Syed Ali Ashraf, "The Inner Meaning of the Islamic Rites: Prayer, Pilgrimage, Fasting, Jihad," in Seyyed Hossein Nasr, ed., *Islamic Spirituality: Foundations* (London: Routledge and Kegan Paul, 1987), 114.

24. Seyyed Hossein Nasr, *The Essential Seyyed Hossein Nasr*, ed. William C. Chittick (Bloomington, IN: World Wisdom, 2007), 87: "When God softens the heart and removes its veils, the heart becomes worthy of being the receptacle of the Divine Peace or *al-sakīnah* (*shekhinah* in Hebrew), for as the Quran says, 'He it is who sends down peace of reassurance (*al-sakīnah*) into the hearts of believers' (48:4)."

25. W. T. Purkiser, *Exploring Christian Holiness*, vol. 1, *The Biblical Foundations* (Kansas City: Beacon Hill Press of Kansas City, 1983), 13.

26. H. Orton Wiley, *Christian Theology* (Kansas City: Nazarene Publishing House, 1940), 1:370.

27. Purkiser, *Exploring Christian Holiness*, 24.

28. The idea of Christian perfection has been misunderstood and misinterpreted by many. "The Greeks had two words which we translate 'perfect.' One meant to make fully ready, the other meant to complete or finish. The former applies to a

person or thing which is quite fitted and thoroughly furnished for its purpose. . . . The second is used to express perfection in the sense of completeness, which results from growth and experience" (Thomas Cook, *New Testament Holiness* [1903; repr., Salem, OH: Schmul Publishers, 1978], 59-60). We can attain the former in our life now; however, the latter will come only when we are glorified. A good illustration of the present possibility of perfection is that of a screwdriver. A carpenter is doing a repair job that requires a Phillips screwdriver of a certain size. If the screwdriver is too big, it won't slot into the screwhead. If it is too small, it won't turn the screw. But if the screwdriver head exactly matches the slots in the screw, the carpenter will note that that particular screwdriver is "perfect." The screwdriver might be old, rusty, have a nicked handle, and other faults, but because it perfectly fits the screw slots, it is the "perfect" screwdriver. So when we do what God wants us to do, we are perfect. And what does God want us to do? Matthew 22:37-39 tells us that the greatest commandment is this: "'Love the Lord your God with all your heart and with all your soul and with all your mind.' This is the first and greatest commandment. And the second is like it: 'Love your neighbor as yourself'" (NIV).

29. In the Old Testament, holiness was frequently associated with the idea of separation. The articles in the tabernacle, Aaron as high priest, the incense offered on the altar—all were separated or set aside for God's use, and as such they were holy (Exod. 30:30–38).

30. Augustine, *Confessions*, bk. 1, chap. 1, in *The Basic Writings of Saint Augustine* (1948; repr., Grand Rapids: Baker Book House, 1980), 1:3.

31. "Colloquium on Holiness," 18.

Chapter 9: Plank Three: Struggle

1. Miller, *Muslims and the Gospel*, 211.

2. Karen Armstrong, *The Battle for God* (London: Harper Perennial, 2004), 37.

3. David Cook, *Understanding Jihad* (Berkeley, CA: University of California Press, 2005), 35. Cook cites al-Bayhaqi, *Zuhd* (Beirut, n.d.), 163 (no. 373).

4. Many people doubt the authenticity of this *hadith,* saying that whenever Muslims talk about jihad, they are talking about the sword.

5. Muhammad al-Bukhari, *Hadith of Bukhari* (repr., n.p.: Forgotten Books, 2008), 560–61.

6. Miller, *Muslims and the Gospel*, 87.

7. Seyyed Hossein Nasr, *The Heart of Islam* (San Francisco: HarperSanFrancisco, 2004), 260.

8. Ayoub, *Islam: Faith and History*, 68.

9. Seyyed Hossein Nasr, *Sufi Essays* (Chicago: ABC International Group, 1999), 77–82.

10. Khan, *Principles of Islam*, 53–54.

11. Wesley, *Works*, 5:412–13.

12. Richard J. Foster, *Celebration of Discipline* (San Francisco: Harper and Row, 1978), 1.

13. Ibid., 7–8.

14. Ibid., 13–171.

Chapter 10: Practical Advice for Bridge Builders

1. Fouad Masri, *Hummus, Haircuts, and Henna Parties* (Indianapolis: Crescent Project, 2009), 16-18.

2. Ibid., 21.

Chapter 11: A Common Word between Us and You

1. A Common Word, "The ACW Letter," 2007, http://www.acommonword .com/the-acw-document/.

2. Ghazi bin Muhammad, "'A Common Word between Us and You': Theological Motives and Expectations," *Sophia: The Journal of Traditional Studies* 14, no. 2 (Winter 2008–9): 7, 14.

3. Ibid., 10.

4. Mahmoud M. Ayoub was born in South Lebanon. He received his education at the American University of Beirut (BA, philosophy, 1964), the University of Pennsylvania (MA, religious thought, 1966), and Harvard University (PhD, history of religion, 1975). From 1988 to 2008, he was a professor and director of Islamic Studies in the Department of Religion, Temple University, Philadelphia; an adjunct professor at the Duncan Black Macdonald Center, Hartford Seminary, Connecticut; a research fellow at the Middle East Center, University of Pennsylvania; and the Tolson visiting professor at the Pacific School of Religion, Berkeley, California.

5. Mahmoud Ayoub, "Christian-Muslim Dialogue: Goals and Obstacles," *Muslim World* 94 (July 2004): 314–16.

6. Ibid.

7. Ibid.

8. Ibid.

9. Ibid., 317–18.

10. Ibid., 318.

11. M. Darrol Bryant was professor of religion and culture at Renison University College, University of Waterloo in Waterloo, Ontario. He is now a distinguished professor emeritus. He is the director of the Centre for Dialogue and Spirituality in the World Religions.

12. M. Darrol Bryant, "Overcoming History: On the Possibilities of Muslim-Christian Dialogue," *Hamdard Islamicus* 17, no. 2 (1994): 9–11.

13. Ibid., 11.

14. John L. Esposito and Dalia Mogahed, *Who Speaks for Islam?* (New York: Gallup Press, 2007). Even after the traumatic events of 9/11, a majority of Americans still know very little about Islam (xiii).

15. Ibid. "A *Washington Post*/ABC News poll in 2006 found that nearly half of Americans—46%—have a negative view of Islam, seven percentage points higher than observed a few months after Sept. 11, 2001" (46).

16. Ibid., 155. Twenty-two percent of Americans say they would not want a Muslim as a neighbor, 32 percent say they admire nothing about the Muslim world, and 25 percent admit they simply don't know much if anything about Muslims.

17. Esposito and Mogahed, *Who Speaks for Islam?* 155.

18. Ibid., 14.

19. Zakaullah, *The Cross and the Crescent*, flyleaf.

www.ingramcontent.com/pod-product-compliance
Lightning Source LLC
LaVergne TN
LVHW051557080426
835510LV00020B/3015